WHAT NOW?

An Honest Guide to Miscarriage, Baby Loss, Parenting, Mental Health and Rebuilding Your Identity.

Clara Wilcox

COPYRIGHT

Title: What Now? An Honest Guide to Miscarriage, Baby Loss, Parenting, Mental Health and Rebuilding Your Identity.

First published in 2018

Published by The Balance Collective c/o 406a Birmingham Road, Sutton Coldfield, Birmingham, B72 1YJ

ISBN 978-1-9165027-0-3 (paperback version)

Book design: Gina Cox-Roberts from The Red Stone Studio

Editing: Chloe Ivy Rose Smith

COPYRIGHT ACKNOWLEDGEMENTS

To all the people that helped piece me back together
and made us love life again

CONTENTS

"And once the storm is over you won't remember how you made it through. How you managed to survive. You won't even be sure, in fact, whether the storm is really over. But one thing is certain. When you come out of the storm you won't be the same person who walked in. That's what this storm is about."

Haruki Murakami

INTRODUCTION

Wednesday 16th June 2010 is etched into our minds forever. The date we discovered that the baby we desperately wanted for years was not going to come home.

That date was the culmination of two years of medical appointments and hospital trips. A rollercoaster that took us from secondary infertility issues and miscarriage to an impending late pregnancy loss. To maternal mental health struggles, depression diagnosis, genetic testing and then, by 8th June 2012, holding our final child in our arms.

Our journey is not unique; it is one that far too many families go through, yet baby loss, fertility issues and mental health are sorely lacking in conversation. At best, it is found in whispered conversations.

When you go through the loss of a baby in pregnancy, especially in the second trimester, you enter a strange no-man's land. People can't really imagine the reality of the loss. You give birth, but you go home alone. If this happens before the end of the twenty-fourth week of pregnancy, you have no parental leave, no birth certificate. Yet you still ache for your loss of YOUR baby.

For our late loss, we had an added level of complication, as we chose to have our little boy at nearly 21 weeks pregnant after we discovered he had Potter's Syndrome. A syndrome that meant he was incompatible with life. No matter how hard we hoped and researched, there was no way to bring him home. No medical intervention would change the inevitable ending. His lack of working kidneys was catastrophic to his development. He would not be able to breathe once he was born. So, we decided to take control of the situation and have him induced, to prevent added distress for us and pain for him.

All in all, it was a shit time.

It was a painful, hysterical, funny, bizarre, loving and shit time.

This is a book filled with hope, raw and honest emotions and the book I needed to read when it happened to me.

But this is not just my story. I have the honour of including the stories of twelve mothers who have shared their journey of loss and grief, and life after loss. What happened to them, how they felt and what they did to find the joy in life again.

I hope it helps you reading it, as much as it has helped me in writing it.

HOW TO USE THIS BOOK

Life doesn't follow a linear path. Regardless of how well we think we have things planned, it doesn't work out this way. What I have covered in here is based on my journey, covering fertility issues, miscarriage, second trimester loss, returning to work as a bereaved parent, mental health, parenting after loss and pregnancy after loss.

You may find you are at different stages in your journey and you may need to skip ahead and read one part more than another. This hasn't been designed to be read chronologically, but by what you may need right now. Your beginning may be my end; so go straight to the final chapter where I talk about how to heal, and what to do practically to move forward. Then do this.

If parts don't resonate with you – just pass over them.

If specific parts are only relevant to your family or friends – then pass this onto them.

What you won't find here is anything religious; this isn't part of our story and didn't offer me any comfort.

What you will find is an honest, yet a little sweary, insight into what worked for us.

KEEP IN TOUCH

As you will gather after reading this book, consistent communication is one of the most important things when overcoming any type of life change. I want us to keep in contact; you'll find out how later.

ONE: DODGING FERTILITY BULLETS

"You don't have to see the whole staircase, just to take the first step"

Martin Luther King

The irony isn't lost on me. That many of us spend most of our adult lives trying to avoid falling pregnant. As a young adult, the utter terror of falling pregnant would haunt me at night. The hormones that I would pump into my body were not only to control my mercurial moods, but to stop me becoming a mum before I was ready.

The horror stories we would read about failing pills and discovering what would interfere with its effectiveness. The hours I would spend whilst at university, volunteering for the free pregnancy testing service where I would hand out sage advice and thankfully, gave the news "it's a negative test" out with every session.

Popping pills to trick your body; panic buying tests if Aunt Flo doesn't arrive when you expect her to.

Then bam, it hits you.

I WANT A BABY.

I NEED TO HAVE A BABY.

It's like my ovaries were twitching at the sight of every small baby I saw.

I had visions of yummy mummy lunches with a well behaved, blue eyed, blonde haired little cherub who sleeps when I need them to sleep and fits like a glove on my hip.

Next, I was researching what I needed to do to get pregnant.

Charting my temperature. Inspecting parts of my body I didn't know existed. Paying attention to cycles and fertility windows and ovulation signs.

Pregnancy number one lulled me into a false sense of fertility security. It appears that coming off the contraceptive pill, for me at least, created a window of uber fertility which meant we didn't need to spend too long trying.

The first time around it all happened like clockwork - the speed of conception surprised us both. Even after a decade of chemical intervention, our joint genetic makeup meant I was pregnant less than two months after I stopped the pill.

The story behind that pregnancy announcement still makes me smile as I write now. With no sign of a period but a negative test, I took myself off to the doctor's one Friday morning in 2005. In the rushed appointment I was told that a messed-up cycle was quite a common part of contraceptive withdrawal. I just had to keep testing until I got a positive or a period.

Great!

Still in a limbo state, I stopped off to grab a chocolate bar and a pregnancy test on the way back to work and in my rush to eat and drive, I managed to drop chocolate all over my trousers.

If memory serves, I tried to eat a flake, in the car, whilst driving.

It was inevitable really that it would end up all over me.

The need to change my clothes combined with the fact I have zero patience, I decided to take the test there and then after my detour.

Two blue lines.

Two. Blue. Lines.

After checking and rechecking the instructions, then viewing the test in every possible light, the reality set in.

I was pregnant!

I'd like to tell you I created an elaborate pregnancy reveal to my other half. All staged, creative, a little trendy, with lots of tears.

As you will come to realise, that's not the way I roll, due to lack of self-control and my "hurry up" nature.

To this day, I'm not one-hundred percent sure what he heard over that phone call. You see, he was abroad at a stag weekend that was well and truly in full swing. He still says that phone call sobered him up quicker than any black coffee.

This began the roller coaster of a decade of parenting and fertility ups and downs.

We had no idea what was coming.

Oh, how naive we were to assume that it would all be as easy as that!

PARENTING GUILT

The guilt that is naturally associated with parenting seems to pre-date getting pregnant.

As soon as you decide you want a baby, you worry about what you are putting into your body. What you are eating and drinking? Are you healthy enough? Do you have the right house? What are the local schools like? Will you get decent maternity or parental leave? Do we want a summer born baby? Do we want a winter born baby?

All these things start before DNA meets DNA.

My parenting life started before the advent of smartphones, Facebook Groups, Mummy Bloggers and Instagram Parenting Influencers; which I feel now puts even more pressure on what we expect of ourselves!

Once I got that positive line, I joined an online parenting forum and chatted about, well, the things you feel you can't ask your friends and family. But it only could be at work, as I didn't have a computer or the internet at home. I had to do my research via *books*.

Remember them?

They hold ALL THE FACTS.

We shared the fears that bubbled under the surface. I became quite obsessed with real life birth stories. At the time (2005) *One Born Every Minute* wasn't a thing, so I made do with watching heavily medicated American women share their birth story on screen.

My eye would also be caught by *anything* that was slightly off-centre. I absorbed information about what could go wrong, I think to try to insulate myself from any potential shock of what could go wrong. I still vividly remember one morning show segment which highlighted a mum who was told she was having a boy, when in fact, a girl appeared from her nether regions.

Even though we were told at our 20-week scan we were having a girl, I refused to wash any baby clothes that were pink until our baby arrived. If only that was all I needed to have worried about!

Do you ever put the same expectations on others that you do on yourself? Look around at the people in your life. What do you expect of them?

As you get older and your journey into parenthood develops and changes, there will be times when you are going to be beat yourself up. Laying on unrealistic expectations about a whole heap of things, when you really should be much gentler on yourself.

So, let's use this book as a full stop in your life. Draw a line under the expectations you have had about your life. If you are reading this now, I know that you have gone through a loss of a pregnancy, of a baby that was loved and wanted the minute that line went blue. As soon as the line read "pregnant". Either way, now is the time to give yourself a break.

Be gentle on how your life is now.

Take some time to see what happens.

To take the pressure off.

To relax. Be kind. Love yourself again.

THE SHOCK OF SECONDARY INFERTILITY

By 2008 our first born, Grace, was an active, funny, and talkative toddler. We were starting to move through the new-born haze of sleepless nights. Many of our weekends involved visiting friends and their new-borns and toddlers. It felt like it was about time we started trying for baby number two. And so many people say two-years is a great gap.

Damn my twitchy ovaries.

I won't bore you with those details; we are all adults after all.

What quickly came to pass was after several months, I wasn't getting pregnant. I've lost count of the money that was spent on ovulations sticks and pregnancy tests and other new, fandangled technology that was meant to help.

Bearing in mind how quickly we got pregnant with our first child, I was a tad arrogant expecting it to be an easy catch the second time round.

Then, it happened. No period. Nothing – from late to where the hell is it?

Yet, test after test was negative.

Nada.

Nothing.

As you can imagine, it was rather confusing. I took myself into the doctor's, demanding the blood test that would declare my fertility. I was expecting to find out I was pregnant from that test. But instead I got poked, probed, and scanned. It turned out I have Polycystic Ovary Syndrome (PCOS) and secondary fertility issues.

PCOS is a bizarre set of symptoms that can, in some cases, lead to fertility issues. For me, the diagnosis came due to a no-show period for four months. This led to blood tests to check my hormone levels and then a funky little ultrasound scan to confirm.

We were told how PCOS impacts fertility. We were also warned that it can lead to an increased chance of miscarriage.

We were told our beautiful little girl may be the only chance we had at being parents.

It was a hard one to swallow, but one that we started to accept.

But that is not where our story ends.

We were referred to the fertility clinic at the local hospital, so we carried on with life whilst waiting for an appointment to come through.

It turns out, the human body is quite an unusual thing.

It turns out, you can get pregnant even when your monthlies don't arrive.

Who knew!

Surprisingly, I have a tell when I'm pregnant.

Milk, specifically milk and tea. The combination makes me gag; I can't have it around me.

So, when I found myself turning my nose up at my daily milky cuppa, I knew something was up.

This time around, the pregnancy test went positive very quickly. This was a time before smartphones and internet in the house. I ended up on the NHS helpline checking if PCOS can give you a positive pregnancy test.

Turns out, only the pregnancy hormone hCG can give you a positive pregnancy test.

We were over the moon; we told a few people but decided to hold off from telling my best mates as we were due to go to their wedding. We didn't want to make the day about anything apart from them!

I discovered that I did a good job at hiding how sick I felt, carrying round snacks in my rather trendy clutch bag to reduce the ongoing feeling that I needed to be sick.

When we gave them the good news, the next morning after the wedding, I realised what a good actress I am! Not only had no one noticed that I had nursed the same glass of wine all night, my friends thought I was drunk. I had discovered you could dance the nausea away.

There is no doubt that even at the beginning, pregnancy number two felt different. As I hadn't expected to get pregnant, as we hadn't been "trying", I hadn't started with all the usual pills and potions. No folic acid. No vitamins. There may have even been a few cheeky glasses of fizzy stuff before we got the positive test. Unfortunately, my behaviour before I knew the positive result came back to haunt me in my darker days in the worst possible way.

TWO: THE BULLSHIT TWELVE-WEEK RULE

"We all have an unsuspected reserve of strength inside that emerges when life puts us to the test"

Isabel Allende

I am not quite sure where the twelve-week rule came from. It is just something that was instinctively there, like the other strange rules we have come to live by.

Don't swim after eating.

Don't wear a black bra with a white top.

Not to start eating until everyone's food arrives. Or is that just me who has an issue with that one?

Not to tell anyone that you are pregnant until you are twelve-weeks gone.

Because if you tell people you are going to jinx it.

Right?

The irony is, for our first, pregnancy, we announced it to the world the minute we saw that BFP (for those that haven't spent time on online forums, that acronym is the coveted Big Fat Positive pregnancy test).

In fact, we not only announced it to our friends and family, via text message: namely *"The Wilcoxes are proud to announce that Scott isn't a Jaffa"* (as in seedless orange type fruit); I told my boss too.

I told my boss and our nearest and dearest before the twelve-week mark, and the world didn't fall apart.

I was sick and tired in the first twelve weeks; I needed people to know why I wasn't on form.

I visited a spa the day after I got my positive and had to let them know what I could or couldn't do for health and safety purposes.

I was over the moon to discover my best mate was pregnant too; we shared our joy and discussed, at the chippy, if we could have mayonnaise (that was around the time when we started to get random food advice).

PANIC STATIONS

Ironically, out of all my pregnancies and their issues, my first was the only one that showed any signs of trouble.

I was aware of the things that I should look out for. When you become pregnant, you pay attention to your body in ways you never imagined. The several times a day "knicker check" is least of your worries.

My pregnancy with my firstborn, Grace, was textbook until nearly nine weeks, when I had a bleed one Friday at work. At the time I was a Branch Manager of a Recruitment Consultancy. Just before I was due to interview a candidate I had a massive bleed. I had to sit through that ninety-minutes interview dealing with the internal mantra of *"I'm losing my baby. I'm losing my baby."* all whilst asking the candidate about their key experience and skills.

It wasn't my best work. I still managed to find them a job though! But I digress.

I couldn't get to see anyone until the Monday and, whilst the bleeding had stopped, I had resigned myself to the fact I was having a miscarriage.

The doctor's appointment had temporarily reassured us that, after peeing on a stick, there was still pregnancy hormone in my system, so there was still a chance I was pregnant. If I hadn't already shared our news with my boss, then the Monday morning rush to the Early Pregnancy Unit to await a scan would have been impossible.

There it was (as we had NO idea what flavour child we were having) floating around my womb like a tadpole with a flashing white beating heart.

"9 weeks.5 days. Viable foetus." I've still got that piece of paper in her baby box.

Fast forward four years, we were waiting in the Scanning Unit of the same hospital, excited about seeing Baby Number Two.

We had a rocky start, Number Two and I: being diagnosed with PCOS, being told it was unlikely that I would get pregnant, then getting pregnant without having a period. Mother Nature liked to mess with my head.

Despite this, we were excited to see our baby and were waiting to get a more accurate idea of when I was due.

The thought of pregnancy had appeared a little over a month previously. The tell-tale sign of being mortally offended by the smell of milk and tea (an evil combination) made me take a pregnancy test.

The positive pregnancy test led to a confused call to NHS Direct to ask if PCOS could lead to a positive pregnancy test.

"No, dear," was the reply. *"A pregnancy leads to a positive pregnancy test."*

So, there we were, excited to find out what the future held. Sitting in the waiting room, we discussed our plans. We had already chosen names, planned to move our then three-year-old into a bigger room so that she wouldn't be jealous when baby arrived and eventually had the nursery.

I had even turned down the chance of a promotion opportunity at work, because, you know, *pregnancy* (more on the last point later).

Like before, we had told close family and friends. There were only so many times I could be driving on a night out or being treated with an antibiotic-related illness. I think people were starting to guess!

My name was called; we were prepared. Hey, we were old hands at this, making sure we had enough money to cover the ever-increasing cost of scan pictures to show our little girl she was about to become a big sister.

In we went to the darkened room, full of technology; the cold jelly was smothered on. I laid back and waited to see that little tadpole again.

Instead, the screen was still. The sonographer went quiet.

A quick adjustment and she tried again. Moving the wand to get another angle. Just to make sure.

Because of what had happened a few years before, we knew what we were meant to see at that stage.

"I'm sorry," she said, *"There is no heartbeat."*

I won't lie, I'm not one hundred percent sure what she said after that.

I can tell you what I felt.

Shock.

Heartbreak at the loss.

Disbelief about the lack of drama.

All those things wrapped up into the fact that our baby's heart had stopped beating several weeks before. Probably around the time I stopped feeling sick. Around the time when I was relieved I could get up and not dry heave over a toilet bowl. At that moment, the little one ceased to be. Now according to the bullshit rules of the world, we had jinxed that pregnancy by letting people know.

RULE BREAKERS

How, in a world where we can map DNA, send invisible information in the air and land on the moon, do we *still* follow this ridiculous notion?

Let's be blunt. With approximately seventy-five percent of miscarriages occurring in the first three months of pregnancy, when we get pregnant, there is a very good chance it will not end well.

This is a hard and fast fact of life.

And it's shit.

But it's true.

Having this "rule" supports another fallacy. The idea that once you get to twelve-weeks everything is going to be OK. Well, I and many of you reading this book know this isn't the case.

For those that suffer first-trimester loss, it can be harder to talk about what has happened when we haven't even told anyone we were pregnant in the first place. At the very time where parents-to-be are at their most vulnerable, when they are heartbroken and hurting, we are having to introduce the concept of *"I was pregnant, now I am not."*.

What if we start to make a change?

To talk about pregnancy, with the people we are most comfortable with, as soon as WE SEE FIT.

To share our losses to help others feel less alone.

To stop the assumption that we have any control about what happens.

Step away from the search engines. You will be trying to find answers; I know I was. Was it the big bottles of water I carried? The initial lack of folic acid? The glasses of wine I had before I knew? I found a link between PCOS and loss, as well as lots of crazy and ridiculous things, even panicking about the episode of a slapped cheek in the family!

Whilst all losses have a reason, you need to understand, *they are out of your control.*

If your loss is raw, it may sting a little to read this.

I am writing this nearly ten years on from my first loss.

There is 89.75585 percent chance that if I read this, back then, I would tell myself to take a long walk off a short pier.

WE HAVE LOST OUR BABIES.

We have lost a future, fully imagined at the very moment the test went positive.

But it isn't anyone's fault.

It doesn't help that, at the very time we want answers, the medical professional can't give them to us.

What stung the most for me, with our first loss, was how everyday it was.

We were given a few leaflets on miscarriage. They explained what may happen next, then escorted us out the back door of the Maternity Unit by a sympathetic, but slightly frazzled looking, midwife.

I don't think we had any real time to process it. The doctor went through the ways we could manage the pregnancy; naturally or medically. A shrug of the shoulders and reassurance that there is no reason it would happen again. I would need to lose two more, before they would investigate any further.

The only thing they would check was if the pregnancy was a rare molar pregnancy, where there is no embryo, just a bundle of cells. Discovering a molar pregnancy can lead to months of treatment and possibly chemotherapy, due to the 'rogue cells', so we waited with bated breath for the results. Luckily, we got the all clear. But it meant that we had lost our second child.

We already had one healthy child. We just had to accept we were now a statistic.

Sound familiar?

THREE: MY TRUTH ABOUT MISCARRIAGE

"You aren't what's happened to you, you are how you have overcome it"

Beau Taplin

Until this had happened to me, I had only witnessed miscarriages through films and TV. All drama and flashing lights.

What I didn't expect was a gently spoken, slightly bored-looking doctor asking me if I was going to wait for nature to take its course at home or come in for surgery, and if I needed a medical note to take to work.

I remember sitting at home, too scared to move, just in case it would encourage the miscarriage to happen naturally or increase the inevitable pain. I made the decision to go into surgery a few days later. I couldn't bear the idea of having my little toddler witnessing anything. And, I'm quite comfortable telling you, I was petrified that the miscarriage would start before we got the hospital.

Scared of what I would see.

Scared of how it would feel.

Scared of the pain.

Even with all the information that is out there, from websites to flyers to forums, no one tells you what it feels like. You have a high level of anxiety and panic anyway, and then you spend the next week searching 'does PCOS cause a miscarriage' and 'should miscarriage be this painful?'

It is a physical act. No matter how much I hoped that being put under by a rather smooth-talking Anaesthesiologist would be the end of it, it wasn't.

It's painful.

It's messy.

It's emotional. But, I promise you, it eventually becomes a memory that won't scar you for life.

I hope to the very core of my bones that this never happens to you again.

What I want to share with you, *are my observations*, to try and give you some heads up and hopefully reassure you that what you are going through isn't strange or problematic.

It will hurt, and you will bleed for at least a week

Take the pain relief you are offered. Take the sick note from the doctors to give yourself time to physically and emotionally recuperate. Regardless of the circumstances around your pregnancy and the emotional sliding scale you are on, there are hormonal changes happening. If, like me, you go through a medical route, the General Anaesthetic on its own knocks you about, as does everything else that can happen afterwards.

If you decide to go down the natural route, things may take a little longer. Let the important people around you know what has happened. Be gentle on yourself and make sure you have the time and space to recover and say goodbye.

You can talk about it

Remember, *whenever it happened*, you can talk about it. Don't bottle it up. Don't pretend. Don't avoid. At first, I only really spoke to a couple of people about our missed miscarriage; it was several months on that my whereabouts during that unexpected week off work was discussed. But I had a couple of people that asked me how I was, who were open to my tears and my frustrations and my processing of it all. And you know what? They had guessed what was going on anyway. How? They had been through it themselves! They recognised the signs.

Ask questions

If, like it was for us, this has come as a shock (as often happens with missed or silent miscarriages, where there are no signs that the pregnancy has stopped progressing), you may find that you are given a lot of information in a short space of time. As time progresses you may have more questions and no one to speak to. There are some wonderful charities and organisations out there that you can call and ask. Make sure you check out the resources later on in the book to find out those that are close to you or exist online.

LIGHTENING CAN'T STRIKE TWICE, RIGHT? NO TWO LOSSES ARE THE SAME

I felt like the miscarriage had marked our cards. Closed off a chapter, where my fertility was questioned and under the microscope. I thought the miscarriage meant we had received our share of heartbreak, that we were now clear to "pass go" and feel confident that the powers that be would be kind, gentle, and sympathetic.

I honestly believed this. The pragmatic, level-headed, scientific, atheist, feminist had decided that somewhere, somehow, this horrible experience would protect us against future issues. It was our shield, because no one would be unlucky enough to have this happen to them more than once.

Spot my naivety?

I think this is where the lack of conversation about baby loss did the most damage for me. Whilst it is reassuring when the doctors, the leaflets, and the online forums tell you multiple miscarriages are rare, it doesn't often happen the same way as their positive rainbow birth stories reflect.

This is not said to scare you – it is to tell you should heartbreak strike you again, don't use it as proof that there is something wrong with you or your parenting potential.

Reading about some of the wonderful parents that have contributed to this book, who have had multiple losses, I now see how lucky we are. I have only lost fifty percent of my pregnancies. For some, that number may feel shocking, at two in four, but that is actually pretty good odds. At the time that we had our first loss we had the confidence, upfront, to know that I *could* conceive and bring a baby into the world. There are many, many couples that haven't had such a clear-cut journey to creating their family.

So, very simply, if you are on the multiple losses train, or your loss is anything apart from "text book" (in the eyes of medical professionals), I wholeheartedly encourage you to take as many tests as they will offer you. It may not give you answers straight away, but it can eliminate some of the more common issues that can lead to miscarriage. The information about your losses is data that can be used by the medical profession to help you eventually bring your baby home. And, on a practical level, these tests can lead to the opportunity to access the support you may need now or in the future.

We were open to as many tests as we could get our hands on, and as you will find out later in the book, these tests may have led to a happy ending and medical advancements.

I DON'T WANT TO BE PART OF THIS EXCLUSIVE CLUB

The bullshit twelve-week rule, ongoing taboo about baby loss, and even the topic of death itself, means that we don't talk about grief nearly enough. I get it. What we have been through is worse than terrible. So terrible that I have struggled through a thesaurus to find a single word that can describe how it feels.

All I can describe is a sound.

It was a rush of emotion and an internal scream that went through my head. It appeared again, during my third pregnancy, when we again discovered our baby wouldn't be coming home.

With pregnancy number three (loss number two) I had started to tell people at around sixteen weeks. Partly due to the, I quote, "*so far so good*" private scan at fourteen-weeks, and partly as my stomach was giving it away. The pregnancy waddle kicked in at about fifteen weeks.

So, when I trotted in to work on Tuesday, 15th June 2010, the day before our anomaly scan, I remember thinking that there could be nothing that could cause real problems. We had not only got past the 'magical' twelve-weeks stage, we had a wonderful scan showing healthy legs and toes and kidneys, when I was nearly fourteen weeks pregnant. The irony is, the kidneys that caused all the problems, that made him incompatible with life, had appeared healthy at that stage.

I had a meeting with a new recruitment client on the Tuesday afternoon, and shared the exciting news as part of that meeting. She had spotted the bump! I had to then phone into work about an issue we were having with a client who, apparently, didn't understand UK employment laws. With a cheery, "*see you tomorrow afternoon*", I went home, excited.

Even now, I remember those days so clearly. I often go back over it in my head, watching it like a film, wishing I could have bottled the happiness I felt at the potential of life on that day.

On the 16th June, the rug was pulled from under us. We were told our baby was not going to survive; that the lack of kidneys meant that every practise swallow and breathe was depleting the life-giving amniotic fluid. You may not know, as I didn't at the time, that the amniotic fluid is more than just a cushion around our little ones. It is an essential part of the physiological development of the baby. In our little boy's case, his lack of working kidneys meant he couldn't just 'pee out' the fluid that he was swallowing. The lack of fluid would not only restrict his growth, but it meant he would run out of the fluid he was breathing in to inflate his lungs. No developed lungs, no ability to breathe once he was born.

I negotiated with the doctors, surgeons, and specialists; in what felt like a modern age, there must have been a way they could have saved our boy. However hard we pleaded there was no hope, and so, on the 20th June 2010, we went into our local hospital to have him.

I was so emotional broken I hadn't really paid any attention to the Consultants instructions, so we made our way straight to the Maternity Ward rather than the Delivery Ward. I found the first person remotely medical looking and told him I was there for my induction. With a glance at my small bump, he responded something like "*Why, you aren't pregnant enough?*" As I told him why we were there, a look of utter horror crossed his face and he apologised and asked us to take a seat. I still hope to this day I didn't upset him too much.

We were directed to the Delivery Ward and we were led to the Bereavement Suite. A room as far away as possible from the other labouring mums, and the induction began.

I won't go into the nitty gritty about the birth. Partly, to be honest, because I was dosed up to my eyes on Morphine and can't remember too much. It's a fact that the human memory is selective at the best of times, even more so when it's high on what is technically a Class A drug. But what I will share with you is what I learnt from the experience.

It took about twelve hours from start to finish to give birth to our little boy. It was painful.

Scrap that, it was excruciating.

Not only did my body not want to give up my little boy, my heart did not want to either. And I am a stubborn fucker when I have made my mind up. But, like any pain, I don't remember that much now. The human body and brain have a great way of making sure you block it out.

I had full access to drugs. Because of the pregnancy gestation, I had been warned there may be, what they called, "*signs of life*". But, because I was less than 22 weeks pregnant, they couldn't "*put baby to sleep*". It was a horrific choice; do I wait a few weeks longer to make sure he isn't in pain during the birth? Or have him now and risk it? Scott and I had spoken, and I asked the Midwife to pass the baby to Scott, should there be any. However, the midwife let me know that the morphine that would be available to me would cross over through the placenta and let him drift away peacefully. This is hard to write, but I want to let you know this. Just in case you did the same thing. WE MADE THE RIGHT CHOICE.

We didn't find out he was a boy until he was born; the scans up until then were not clear enough to tell, since they were concentrating on finding a chink of medical hope in his condition. We had a name ready, Callum. The Midwife was so gentle and loving, talking about him as if he was a live birth, and allowed us to spend time as a family. Using his name. Pointing out his tiny finger nails, and his long legs. Our little boy stayed with us all night, as the room and his cot were chilled. We slept fitfully, Scott on a day bed and me in the bed in which I had given birth, weighed down by our grief and shock.

Before this happened, the thought of spending time with my dead baby horrified me. I used the word traumatic when I read about cuddle-cots and saw pictures of children that passed. But this is the part of his birth that I remember so fondly. We got to hold him, dress him, bathe him. Talk to him. We did everything we did with our first-born Grace, pictures included, and those memories are some of the most precious to me.

Leaving the hospital the next day was one of the hardest things we have ever had to do. I am crying as I remember, handing over our little boy, in his tiny Moses basket, to the Midwife. She promised me she would take good care of him before he made his way down to the Funeral Directors. I wanted to run back so many times, to grab him in my arms and take him home. But we had to leave him there; to have gone through all of that and leave the Unit with empty arms felt so unfair.

As I walked out the hospital, alongside parents with their children in car seats, I felt like the world had stopped turning. I had no idea what was to come for us as a couple, as a family, or for me. What I never expected was to be carrying our little girl out of the same place less than two years later.

TALKING ABOUT OUR BABY IN THE REAL WORLD

So, just before I went back to work, after going on bereavement leave for nearly five weeks, I made it clear I wanted my colleagues to know what had happened; there is nothing worse that whispers and rumours. I tried to soften the blow by emailing to let people know I was back, and that whilst I wasn't OK, I was happy to talk about what had happened. Even then, I was trying to make this easier for others rather than protect myself.

The openness to discuss things had an interesting reaction. It encouraged colleagues to share their losses. It made me realise how many parents are carrying losses as part of their lives. People who I had only ever had a civil, professional relationship with started stopping me in the corridor to share their well wishes and their experiences. It was heart-breaking but provided me with some comfort. I wasn't as alone as I felt.

I recall one staff member, who I had worked alongside for several years and *really* intimidated me, delaying the start of our official meeting whilst she spent nearly thirty minutes sharing with me not only the delicate and heartfelt details of the baby she lost, but the impact it had on her future pregnancies.

So, so many parents have these stories bubbling at the surface, waiting for an opportunity to talk about it. Why is it that the only permission we have to share is when another person has gone through it?

I often say how lucky I am to have experienced these losses during a digital revolution. To have forums where I could find people, any time of the day or night, to chat about what I felt. To anonymise my name and face so I could rage against the world, in text form, whenever I felt the need.

The irony is, as I look back, I can count on one hand the people that I knew in real life, that I could draw this support from at the time.

Once you get the access all areas pass to the world's worst club, it can draw an invisible line in the ground between those that have and those that haven't.

Let's be clear. No money, status, or fame can protect people from baby loss. Even the heights of wealth and the medical care it can provide can't stop it happening, once, twice, or more.

I found myself reading about people in the public eye that had gone through baby loss. I got a little obsessed at the time to see who else this had happened too. I needed someone to measure my recovery against.

What I have found is that the way in which celebrities deal with it varies; some are very public at the time, pouring their loss into their music or art, and some start backing charities and become vocal about the support they were given.

They, like us, are struggling with joining a club they never wanted to be part of.

Annie Lennox's take on the stillbirth of her son in 1988 sums it up:

> *"It had an immense impact on me. It made me realize that the human condition is immensely fragile and strong at the same time."*

FOUR: LET'S TALK ABOUT GRIEF

> *"Grief is like the ocean; it comes in waves, ebbing and flowing. Sometimes the water is calm, and sometimes it is overwhelming. All we can do is learn how to swim."*
>
> *Vicki Harrison*

How can you love someone you have never met?

How can you grieve someone that you have never known?

I'm the first to admit that, until it happened to us, I had no idea. I was, and still am, a logical and practical person. Yes, this experience has softened my edges, but I still have the heart of a scientist.

I think, for most people that haven't experienced baby loss, this is often the hardest thing to explain. That the minute the test shows a positive, you have a new future mapped out. With names and imagined personalities.

When you are told your baby has passed, irrespective of how pregnant you were, or why (if you ever get a reason), you are grieving a future you never got to have. The potential of the life that you have imagined.

I often talk about the amazing late 1990's film *Sliding Doors* (Not seen it? Sort it out, pronto). In this, Gwyneth Paltrow plays a character whose life hinges on whether she catches a train – it goes without saying, she has no idea of the importance of catching that train – and we view the way her life plays out, in parallel.

That is how it works with baby loss, yet we witness our sliding door moment in heart wrenching slow motion and confusion. To watch that future disappear in a few moments, it is then very hard to understand what we are meant to do next.

WHAT IS GRIEF?

I am hoping what I will share with you now is not brand-new information. That you will have heard about grief through support from the hospital or another bereavement organisation. However, in the research for this book, and reading the stories of other bereaved parents, it has become quite clear how patchy the support is, not only just across the UK but further afield.

Now, before I go any further, a disclaimer. My qualifications to talk about this come predominately from my lived experience. I do have a background in Psychology; from my degree many moons ago and my ongoing qualifications in Coaching and Mentoring. So, I draw on all these things, plus my love of research and reading, to present this chapter on grief.

Grief is a natural response to losing something; it is the reaction to experiencing a bereavement. You are mourning something that was important to you. From the future you imagined, to the bond created with the little one through little kicks, you are grieving what is no longer there.

For many of us, this loss comes out of the blue. Both of my losses hit me harder than all the bereavements that I had experienced as I had no idea. No sign, no expectation. Even if it is something that was predicted or there were warning signs, the reality of it happening is a shock.

How you may respond to the loss can be influenced by lots of things: your religious or spiritual beliefs, your support network, and your health can all impact how this grief is exhibited. Regardless of how your feelings show up, they are *all* valid.

For many of us we are expected to or needed to return to some form of 'normality' not long after the loss. It may sound harsh, but I noticed a hierarchy of sympathy with my losses. The first, in the first trimester, was chalked up to experience and bad luck. For my second, at nearly twenty-one weeks, our baby was given a name and a funeral and I was allowed, for a certain amount of time, to grieve.

I had the assumption that my grief for the loss of the pregnancies, the loss of my children, would show up the way that it arrived the last time I had a bereavement, when I lost my Grandparents. But it didn't.

And that is what threw me. I had no idea what I was meant to do next.

When people talk about grief, there is often the aim to get to a point when you can accept it. Now, don't for one minute assume that acceptance is being OK or happy with what has happened. It is getting to a place that you can live with the fact that this has happened, as it becomes your new normal.

What is important to realise is that grief can appear and remain in your life in a range of ways that you may not associate with grief. It could be the headaches that constantly arrive and rarely fade away, feeling confused, struggling at work, numbness, anger, frustration or anxiety. None of these include feeling sad. This is because grief is so much more than feeling upset.

For my first miscarriage, it goes without saying that I was sad, but I was quite quickly able to reset my mind to the life we were going to have, continuing as a family of three, not four. There were times later that year, where I would realise how pregnant I should have been by then, and a feeling of relief would pass by. I was so settled into the life that we had, I felt like a baby wouldn't have been the best option for us. Whilst that was tinged with a little guilt, it was an indication that I had worked my way through what had happened and that I had accepted it.

Because of this, I assumed I had this grief thing down, and I now had a way of handling anything else that was thrown at me.

Oh, if only it was that easy!

THE STRANGE WAY GRIEF MAKES YOU BEHAVE: WHERE IS THE RULE BOOK?

Since I started writing this book, I have been discussing the past with some of my closest friends. What they noticed when they witnessed what we went through, particularly our second later loss. About how I was and how I dealt with the loss of the little boy we called Callum.

The most common theme that came up?

That I suppressed so much at the time. That I wasn't in a good place.

This is something that really surprised me. For the most part, I thought I had expressed myself well, and dealt with it in a methodical and logical way. At least, until I became depressed.

Yeah, maybe, on reflection, I didn't deal with it all that well.

Grief plays with your mind. It plants seeds of doubt and uncertainty, and even before my strings of mental wellness fell apart, it broke apart what was routine and predictable for me. I didn't know how to grieve, especially when we lost our little boy. You get leaflets, but they didn't teach me how to grieve in these circumstances. I understood all the theory. But it wasn't quite working for me.

Where can you get your 'Baby Loss Manual' to tell you what you are meant to do? None of us know how to behave when you are grieving a baby that doesn't technically have an identity beyond what you have created for them. We're not told how to cope with a loss that has a funeral but no recognition of existence in the eyes of the law.

This was a time of turmoil for me, a time of breaking apart and starting again. What you will find in the rest of this book is a 'warts and all' guide to what I did, an impartial as possible look at what worked, and what didn't and finally, my thoughts on how you can help yourself through this time in your life.

I'll start with the funny side, just to lighten the mood a little.

The brain can react quite strangely when the rug is pulled from under it.

As I had no idea how to cope with what had happened, I tended to overthink things. The generally bizarre things that occurred, in the early days, included:

Not wearing makeup

There was a logic behind this. Makeup, to me, is part and parcel of a celebration. I *had* to look sad. I felt that if I wore makeup then somehow it would be disrespectful, and people would think I wasn't upset. It wasn't a lack of personal care, more that I had to wear the face of a mourner. Strangely, in previous situations where I have been very upset, I would use the makeup to cover up how I was feeling.

Being worried I'd be spotted out and about

I clearly remember having to venture into Birmingham City centre to return a pair of maternity jeans and a toy we had bought when I was pregnant. I look back now and smile at the *Mission Impossible* secret agent approach that I took, as I was worried that I'd be criticised for shopping. The thing is, I would never think badly of anyone who was out and about after a loss, so the fact I assumed anyone would think the worst of me shows the way my brain was working.

Making strange connections to things that aren't at all connected

To maintain my 'not going outside' strategy, I did my grocery shopping online. However, I managed to get stuck with forty-seven bananas; ordering seven bunches rather than seven individual ones. I made banana bread. Lots of it. As this happened after both losses, I decided for a while that, whilst delicious, banana bread was associated with death. So, I wouldn't buy them.

Rather than realise it was a common mistake, and that I was otherwise distracted, I made this connection. Somehow it was an omen, and I would be suspicious of banana bread for many years. Yes, I realise now how ridiculous it sounds now it is written in black and white (and if you are wondering, the curse of the banana bread has since been broken!).

Working hard to make other people feel comfortable

Rather than worrying about my own feelings, I would be too conscious of how sharing my discomfort and our loss would affect other people. This would include apologising if I got upset, saying things like "It's OK, these things happen," when they said how sorry they were and feeling unsure how to answer the question "How many children do you have?"

I would overeat

I would eat a lot in secret. That is the first time I have typed this, and do you know what, the world hasn't fallen apart. My sugar rush was my comfort. Luckily it was a crutch that I could get through and didn't have long term implications on my health and wellbeing; just my wardrobe and my bank balance.

This is just my list, and this is just the list that I acknowledge was strange. However, these were all behaviours that were my coping mechanisms. You will have your own. They will change and evolve as time passes, but to stay healthy, you must always pay attention to yourself.

Look at what you are doing and thinking and ask yourself "*how is this helping me?*"

If you can't find a way this is helping you, then consider if it's doing more damage to you than good.

You may find it isn't something that you can answer yourself. Talk to someone you trust. Tell them what is going on in your head! Help them pick apart the jumble that may be consuming you.

Sometimes I annoy myself about how deep I get into the nuts and bolts of how the human brain works. This was my security blanket through our baby losses. I couldn't find any reason for why it happened, so instead I found reasons for why I felt like I did.

Our second loss, the one that really pulled the earth from under our feet, marked the start of a long journey of investigations; not only having our DNA and medical history pulled apart to find reasons, but I deconstructed myself.

What I knew, without a doubt, was that I was grieving. And what I understood, without apology, was that I had the right to grieve.

My way.

But what is grief? Let's hand this part over to the Scientists.

THE GRIEF CURVE

One of the pioneers of the Psychology of Grief was Elisabeth Kubler-Ross, who published one of the most recognised theories named 'The Grief Curve'. It was first published in the book *On Death and Dying* and was inspired by her work with terminally ill patients. She believes that there are five stages of grief that people move through; usually people experience at least two, but not necessarily in the order that are presented.

These are: *denial, anger, bargaining, depression,* and *acceptance.*

Writing this book has made me really reflect on and unpick my emotional reaction to our loss. I think the biggest thing that worked for me was to eventually focus on what I had, not what I'd lost; this helped me work through the five stages to a point of acceptance. In fact, I think I skipped straight from *denial* to *anger* (why did it happen to us?), to *bargaining* (what could I have done to change it?), to *depression* (what have we missed out on?), to *acceptance* (this is just the way it needs to be).

GROWING AROUND GRIEF

I recently saw a wonderful example of grief that I know rings true for me, and I hope it will eventually for you.

Lois Tonkin has an alternative model of grief, called Growing Around Grief. Here, the belief is the grief becomes smaller over time in comparison to the rest of your life. At first, the grief is all encompassing and all consuming, filling up every element of our lives. However, eventually the person grows around their grief, their experiences and their life expand around it. Whilst the grief doesn't change, the person grows around it so that is becomes a smaller, but still as intense, part of them.

The message is simple. Grief becomes a part of who you are, but it doesn't define you.

And you don't just "*get over it*". You absorb it.

I remember thinking, after losing our little boy, that I would never feel happy again. It was like all the joy had been sucked out of my life, and I had lost the ability to understand what it felt like. It was crippling.

To be sat here writing this now, having experienced some amazing, life-changing highs, I know that I have grown around the grief.

THE DUAL PROCESS MODEL OF GRIEF

In the world of psychological theories of grief, the Dual Process Model of Grief by Margaret Stroebe and Hank Schut is one of the newbies.

What I really like about this model, unlike a lot of the others that are more commonly discussed, is that it acknowledges the male experience of type of grief.

When we lost our two babies my husband's experience of grief and loss was very different. Not only was he expected to be my support, he wasn't really acknowledged in any of the support I was offered. Combined with an expectation of how we *should* grieve, it can lead to an unhealthy way of processing loss.

Stroebe and Schut gives us all hope. The model is a dual process, following two ways of grieving, which is task-based and changes all the time.

Basically, your everyday life can and will move between feeling the loss caused by the bereavement with what they call *Restoration Orientated* experience.

So, in plain English, one day you can feel devastated about the loss, feel sad and overwhelmed. Then you may find you pick yourself up and think about the new things that you need or want to do. Then, you may move back to burying your head in the sand.

THIS IS NORMAL.

It is not a sign that you don't care.

It is not a sign that you can't cope.

It is not a sign that you are in denial.

This is the way our emotional systems balance out the duality of loss and grieving.

Like those sliding doors we talked about before.

So, when you sit and reflect on how you are feeling now, which of the above theories makes sense to you? How can you use what you have uncovered to make sense of your feelings?

Post-Traumatic Growth Theory

So many people that I talk to that have gone through a loss like we have say how they feel stronger now. Maybe, like me, it's about risk taking? When we tried new things and took chances where we wouldn't have before, we grew stronger.

For others, it may be changes in their life. Moving to a new house, changing jobs, changing partners; big overhauls in their life.

The scientist in me finds it fascinating why this seems to happen. There is research around this that may give you hope. If not, it just makes for some interesting reading.

It's called *Post Traumatic Growth Theory.*

First, let's confront the elephant in the room. What we have been through is trauma. It is devastating. We have been through a traumatic loss.

This not to sensationalise what we have been through, or to turn it into a dramatic plot. We have experienced the very definition of a traumatic loss. Cruse Bereavement Care describes traumatic loss as "*when someone who you care about dies in a sudden and/or traumatic situation*".

In the circumstance of our two losses, it was sudden. We had no idea it was coming. We didn't expect it.

How your loss happened may vary and your experience may too. This is not a place to decide what is traumatic but it is to do with acknowledging that we have survived, and will survive, a traumatic loss.

The idea behind Post-Traumatic Growth Theory is, very simply, experiencing a traumatic event, and positively working your way through the difficulty it leaves, and how it helps an individual develop.

Tedeschi says:

> *"People develop new understandings of themselves, the world they live in, how to relate to other people, the kind of future they might have and a better understanding of how to live life,"*

I know that I have certainly changed how I see the world. In some ways, I am more vulnerable that I was before; but generally, I feel I have a pool of strength I never even imagined before. That if I was to speak to the pre-2009 Clara, I would not be speaking to the person I am today.

Why am I sharing this with you? Whilst my Psychology degree has been dusted off for this book, I'm not a psychiatrist or a psychotherapist. I feel very strongly that wherever you are in your journey, there is light at the end of the tunnel. Research like this gives some substance to my personal anecdotes and other experiences you will read about at the end of the book.

You may be reading this book feeling like you are rudderless. That you don't know what to believe any more. How to trust the future you have mapped out for yourself.

The Post-Traumatic Growth Theory offers a glimpse into why you may be feeling this way. Should you walk into the office of a psychologist, they may review how you are progressing through your trauma by asking you how you are feeling about these five areas:

1. Appreciation of life.
2. Relationships with others.
3. New possibilities in life.
4. Personal strength.
5. Spiritual change.

Take some time yourself to think about how you feel about each of these parts of your life.

What areas do you think you need to do some work in?

When I review this now and look back on how my life has developed, knowing about Traumatic Loss and Post-Traumatic Grief Theory has helped me accept my personal journey.

Those moments, mid grief, where I could see a positive from what happened (which, when it first occurred, made me feel like I was the worst person in the world) were indications of this growth. It made me realise it was part of the process of rebuilding, not a reflection on my outlook on the world. I made me consider the part that Post-Traumatic Growth has had on the process of rebuilding a stronger version of me.

IS IT POSSIBLE TO EXPERIENCE GROWTH FROM GRIEF?

Now, I want to pass this part of the book over to Monica Douglas-Clark. She is a spiritual counsellor and Inclusive Interfaith Minister.

It has been important to me that this book is open to all, without a religious slant. But, let's be honest, going through loss like this rocks your belief system, whatever that may be.

It is important to have someone, neutral and understanding, who is comfortable to talk about death and grief, who understand the process and gives you direction and hope.

In this memorial garden,
I grieve and remember it all.
I allow myself to feel.
I open my heart to unlock the love.
I create new growth from the energy that is released.

Monica Douglas-Clark

I remember the sense of guilt, failure, devastation, and rage that I felt after my first miscarriage. The energy trapped in those emotions was also present with my subsequent miscarriage (that I told no one about), abdominal operations and four tortuous IVF rounds. During this time, I felt bereaved from the three souls that moved through me - Ella, Isis and Alexander. I was in deep grief for the hopes and dreams that had been demolished. It broke my heart repeatedly.

My grief included rage at God, the universe and my husband. I even raged at the cat and she hadn't done anything. The emotion that inspired most guilt was jealousy towards my sisters and my family. The year of my first miscarriage was also the year that the five other women of childbearing age in my family conceived and gave birth to healthy, happy babies.

Although on the outside I nodded and smiled at the platitudes and clichés suggesting the, "it's all happening for a reason," when internally I was thinking "how dare anybody suggest that anything useful could come out of all of this?"

Yet at some point, and I couldn't tell you exactly when it was, I also tapped into part of me that decided that I was going to fully experience and transform the conflicting emotions washing through me. I made a pact with myself to reclaim my energy and do something with it.

Whether my losses had happened for a reason, or not, I was going to choose to find some good and growth out of the grief. I took action to grieve consciously. I took time in nature, danced and nourished my soul. I sought help from books, the Internet and most importantly people. I allowed myself to feel and accept all of my emotions. I worked to feel whole, healed and 'more' as a result of my experience rather than 'less than'. I could touch the scars and feel gratitude instead of rage.

Even if you are not ready to hear this yet, I invite you to consider that you can grow from grief. I've experienced and trained in many forms of therapy, practices, ritual, and ceremonies to make peace with grief. These experiences are a key reason why I do the work that I now do, and my world had definitely expanded. I won't pretend that it was easy, but it is possible.

Most experts say that growth can come from grief

Reviews of clinical studies and literature on coping with bereavement demonstrate that post-traumatic growth, described as positive personal changes resulting from trauma, can occur in bereaved individuals. This growth can be present and demonstrated alongside and at the same time as the more usual negative emotions related to grief. (Znoj 2016, Calhoun, Tedeschi, Cann and Hanks 2010)

The practice of experienced grief professionals also indicates that growth or the perception of growth occurs as a result of the work. In her recent book Grief Works, Julia Samuels explains that a purpose of her work as a specialist grief psychotherapist is to "reassure the bereaved that lives can be rebuilt and trust developed". She says, "We may no longer be innocently hopeful, and we may always have times when we feel the pain of loss, but the deeper understanding of ourselves that we have gained will, in time, feel like growth." (Samuels 2018)

Grief gardening a metaphor inspiration from The SANDS Memorial Garden

A very practical demonstration of the possibility of growth from grief, in the context of parental bereavement, is the SANDs (Stillborn and Neonatal Death Charity) Memorial Garden at the National Memorial Arboretum in the centre of England. This garden is dedicated to the lives of stillborn babies and babies who have died shortly after birth. The recognition of grief, sense of hope and possibility for growth is palpable in this space. It can be a useful place, at the right time, for bereaved parents to visit to open up to the possibility of growth from grief.

I often use the metaphor of the grief garden to help people to understand what I do. Please forgive me for the simplicity of the model but I'd like to invite you to reflect with me on this memorial garden as a way to open up to the possibility of growth from grief.

Acknowledge your loss

Acknowledgement is the first stage in the spiritual counselling model of supporting people through the trauma of bereavement. The bereavement or loss has landed like a truckload of rubble, horse dung, and rubbish in the centre of the place that was once a beautiful ordered garden filled with growing plants of hopes and dreams. The known pathways have all been obscured, and it seems impossible to navigate around a space that was once so familiar but now uncharted territory. We look at the devastation and the trauma of the loss. We see, hear and feel the impact that this loss has had and the feelings that have been evoked.

Often in this time there seems no possibility that there can ever be anything useful to come out of this situation. There is no getting around it. It stinks, it's hard work, painful and backbreaking even when you have support and especially if you don't feel strong enough to do it. At this point it may or may not be time for us to roll up our sleeves and deal with sorting out the rubble and the rubbish from the dung.

In the National Memorial Garden, the names of the babies and the experience of the bereaved parents are acknowledged. There are many stones, some unnamed some with names and dedications placed alongside each other to acknowledge the existence and the loss of each baby. Each stone that is placed in the garden gives voice and space to a soul that has come through. These parents know that they are not alone and that they are supported.

Integration – Grieve and come to your own understanding

In *The Light of Death*, Tim Freke, states that "Bereavement… is a life changing experience, the effects of which must be integrated into our character, so that our love and our loss, and the wisdom we have acquired through the grieving process, become part of us." (Freke 2010) Using our gardening metaphor, this is the time for us to clear the ground and sort the rubble and rubbish from the dung. Once the dung is clear we can put it in the hot box to make compost.

Most grief experts and practitioners agree that grief requires work and time. In order to experience growth through grief we are also required to come to a deeper understanding of our character and our capacity to heal, grow and continue to love despite the "apparent meaningless of loss."

This integration stage is focussed on healing the wounds and riding waves of grief to find your own meaning. Through this process it is possible to find the personal relevance that this experience of bereavement and loss brings to your life. It is important to find your own personal understanding of this experience and to honour your unique process. It may be useful to acknowledge that we cannot cognitively rationalise our feelings and that the process of grieving is not linear or neatly packaged into defined stages.

Transform the energy of trauma to grow

The final stage in this process of grief gardening is to release and transform the trauma.

Clara has already mentioned the Tonkin model of growth from grief. In my experience and practice I have seen how it is possible to expand our lives around our loss and open up to new opportunities in life (Samuels, 2018).

In our grief gardening metaphor, we have received clarity, structure and understanding from our grieving process. We transform the dung into compost; lay new raised beds and plant seeds for growth in the future.

Bob Deits, in *Life after Loss,* states that to grow through loss means to:

- Gain new love and reverence for life
- Shift your attention from the ordinary to the quality elements of life
- Find greater awareness of our mutual need for each other and of the sacred dimension of life.

It maybe that people find that they have a renewed sense of their resilience, deeper relationships, emotional connection and expression and sometimes a powerful sense of the spiritual dimensions of life.

The memorial garden demonstrates this concept. At the centre of the garden there is a sculpture of a baby at rest and a single teardrop representing the grief. Yet, the garden is also wild and full of potential for growth at the edges. The shrubs and trees that have been planted outside of the inner circle create space to expand in height and girth to bring texture, vibrancy and beauty to the space.

There is peace inside the garden. The inner experience is honoured and there is also an awareness of new possibilities for new growth. We can nurture the seeds of hope that arise from this life changing experience.

We transform in the face of the trauma of bereavement to know that there is growth to come.

FIVE: MENTAL HEALTH AS A BEREAVED PARENT

> *"Some people believe holding on and hanging in there are signs of great strength. However, there are times when it takes much more strength to know when to let go and then do it."*
>
> *Ann Landers*

Things started to change one wintery Thursday afternoon. I was running late to one of my brain-fillers; a local sugar craft course (because what says recovery more than hand crafted roses, right?) As I was driving, watching my place in the slow-moving traffic, an overwhelming feeling washed over me. It was so strong that I had to pull over and calm down. The thought of getting there last, with all those eyes on me, made me cry with fear. I couldn't do it. I had to turn around and come back to the safety of my home.

This happened not long after we had returned from holiday. Our little boy's due date had fallen in the winter half term of 2010, so we made the decision to go away. I needed to be distracted, exploring somewhere new on the 27th October. His due date. I had expected that after this milestone, being away in a different place, not associated to our little lad, a weight would lift. The date came and went. Nothing. No relief. I still felt the same. This made me feel angry. Back to the internal monologue of *"Why us?"*

By this point it was nearly six months since it had all happened. I felt as if I had used up the accepted mourning period. At the end of the day, it was a medical procedure. People kept reminding me, it was *"for the best"*, but that wasn't enough. I wanted people to see how I was feeling. I needed to wear my pain.

Back home, with the grief counsellor, I mentioned how I had noticed my driving had changed. You know that moment when you get a little too close to another passing car and you feel tingly? A tiny fission of panic? Well, that had stopped. No panic for me. Instead, I commented how *"I wished I could just drive my car into a wall. If I broke my leg, people would see my pain, notice how I feel and leave me alone!"*

Sometimes a throwaway comment is loaded with so much. It could have been so easily missed. I was, and remain, so thankful she was listening.

I see that version of me now as I write. Broken and scared and angry and alone. I can see the twitch of surprise and panic on the Counsellor's face. I'm sure I wasn't the first or last person to say that.

Was it a call for help?

This is something that many people fail to realise. You can be terribly broken inside, yet the world keeps turning. You go to work. You spend time with your family. You cope. Yet you begin to focus your anger and bitterness inwards, instead.

Being told how brave you are doesn't help when you're in a personal crisis. How can you admit you are falling apart? It doesn't make you look like the brave, stoic parent, carrying on despite the devastation.

I obviously felt safe with the counsellor, enough to admit that I wasn't OK. This was a big deal for me. I'm not a very vulnerable person. It was a turning point.

At her insistence, I went to my GP, who gently guided me through the depression checklist. There it was in black and white. I was clinically depressed and prescribed anti-depressants. Me, the strong, smiling, brave (*oh so brave*!) person was told that what I was feeling wasn't a normal part of grieving.

On the outside, I had built a delicate, but convincing, veneer of coping whilst inside I was screaming. A constant chatter in my head telling me I was to blame, that I'd made the wrong decision. I was convinced that somehow, I could have prevented the loss of our little boy.

So many people were telling me how brave I was. How they couldn't have got through it. How amazing it is that I had just "*moved on."*

I am usually the person that people come to for help. To be honest, I sort of pride myself on being the fixer, the helper. But, who helps the helpers?

I felt like I couldn't share how I was feeling, and the more I held these feelings back, the more vivid the nightmares would get. I would often wake up in a cold sweat after a vivid flashback or what felt like an ominous prediction. But I couldn't share those. They got buried even deeper.

It was a vicious circle.

Having regular grief counselling at the hospital where my loss happened replayed it all for me on a weekly basis. Whilst full of best intentions, the counsellor's approach did more harm than good. Every session I would open up and share the raw vulnerability of how responsible I felt yet was told that I *" shouldn't feel that way"*. Let's be straight. I'm a talker. A pathological dissector of things. I needed to go through that process and I was stopped at every turn.

My usual coping methods at times of crisis or change are like many others. I look for things that I can control. I threw myself into work and tried to push out the bad thoughts with new information, filling my days and evenings with new qualifications and skills from project management to cake decorating. I'd seen how life could turn on a pin. I had to try and work out what my life would be now that the new baby wasn't coming.

As well as signing off a post-mortem for our little boy, we had signed off to be poked and prodded ourselves. It was essential for me that I knew, beyond any reasonable doubt, why this had happened. Could it have been prevented? Who was to blame?

This lack of information was fuelling my fear of if we had made a mistake. What if there was nothing wrong with him and he could have survived? I was sick to my stomach in fear that I had killed my baby and experienced this through a recurring nightmare. Over time, the blame turned inwards. The only person I could be angry with was myself.

Every morning I would plaster on a smile. Every morning I would hope there was no one around I knew on my walk from the carpark to work. My daily pause was a lifeline. I could breathe and force a big smile as I walked down the corridor to the office.

I wasn't coping, and I thought no one else could tell. It is only afterwards that I was told it was obvious that I wasn't. I just wish someone would have told me (or maybe, just maybe they did, and I didn't listen?).

What I have found, as time passed, that I was talking to the wrong person. Whilst the grief counsellor was wonderful, she wasn't right for me. Unusually for me, as I tend to have a *"I'm fine, I can cope"* attitude, I had accepted the help with open, welcoming arms, but quickly found she wasn't what I needed. She was gentle, caring, sympathetic and parental, like a loving family member who wanted to take all the pain away. She provided a safe space to talk; although I am pretty sure that if I had turned up and said nothing at each session, that would have been OK.

I needed someone to challenge me, to help me unravel all the tangled thoughts in my head.

I would find, when I was ready to release what I was truly thinking, the response I would get from friends, family and my wonderful auntie-esque grief counsellor was "*you shouldn't think like that"*.

I have learnt, through my own personal development and work, the destructive power of that word.

Should.

Or, in this case,

Shouldn't.

It is wrapped up in expectations and beliefs. When you think about the word should it is usually an idea of expectations. Obligation. Correctness (yes, I've been looking through the Dictionary!).

So, very simply, other people were projecting their beliefs and expectations onto me.

And, with the greatest of respect to all those well-meaning people, I DIDN'T CARE.

And, to be blunt, I still don't care what they think.

Yes, grief and blame are terrible emotions to feel. In an ideal world, all the people that care about us could magically remove all those negative feelings.

I do think it's a cultural thing – it's exceptionally British to not have difficult conversations or confront discomfort. We just hope things will go away if you ignore them enough. But sometimes we just need to have the difficult conversations. I know I did. I had to walk through alternative options. Feeling uncomfortable is part of the healing process. Ironically, confronting the very things that other people didn't want to speak about helped me heal.

If you need to talk, find the person who will listen.

If you don't want to talk, but you need to get it out of your head, find a way. It may be writing, poetry or art. It may be sticking your headphones on and chasing it away on a run.

Find something that works for you and find the time to make it happen. Don't carry it around. It's a toxic weight that can bring you down.

Don't let other people dictate how you get through this. This is your journey not theirs. I honestly believe that if I had just found the right person to speak to earlier, I wouldn't have got so ill.

You need to protect yourself, your emotions and your well-being.

Sometimes that means shouting a little louder than normal.

WHAT IF GRIEF TURNS INTO DEPRESSION?

I felt a bizarre sense of relief when I got my diagnosis of depression. It was quite a simple process once I had made the decision I was going to ask for help. I went in to see the doctor, who gave me a checklist to complete. It was essential I was honest; I could have quite easily lied about how I was feeling, to keep up appearances. But what good would that have done? I was getting desperate.

I had started to be scared that this was me for the rest of my life. Carrying around an internal black cloud, feeling disconnected and detached and angry.

I was offered medication, and I took it. I know some people struggle with the idea of antidepressants. You may feel hesitant if they are offered to you. You may have assumptions about who needs them, or what it means if you take them. For me, they helped me stabilise. They grounded me and steadied me enough to take on board the other support I needed.

The other support was talking therapy and I was referred to an amazing Bereavement Charity called Edward's Trust in Birmingham.

The combination of chemicals and chatting has meant I am here, writing this today. I honestly believe the combination of the two saved my life. I was heading to a place that wasn't healthy and I wasn't reaching out to speak to people.

There is such a misconception about what depression looks like and, like baby loss and miscarriage, it's considered a taboo. Behaviours and symptoms of depression vary from person to person.

I always assumed that depression would feel like sadness, that I wouldn't get dressed, or socialise, or eat. What I didn't expect was to carry on, day to day, with a dullness, combined with anxiety and frustration. Even with my degree in Psychology, this was something I didn't see coming.

I also didn't expect my first visit to Edward's Trust to make such a difference. My experience of counselling up to that point was that it didn't work; it would just rehash the emotions every week, only to be told that I shouldn't think that way.

I needed something different!

Up to that moment, I blamed myself. I felt like the decision to have our boy early rested solely on my shoulders. I had done what many people do in these circumstances; surrounded myself with information and pictures and tried to find out who else had gone through what we had gone through. All I could seem to concentrate on were those parents that had chosen to go full term with their children, even though they had life-ending issues. Whilst they hadn't taken them home, they had left the outcome up to nature.

I had explained this to my first counsellor, the one that was linked to the maternity unit at the hospital, She, like all the other well-intentioned people, told me I couldn't have done anything different, and I shouldn't feel guilty. Being told that repeatedly, ironically, makes the self-blame worse. After a while, you stop sharing how you feel, and all that blame is focused internally.

Maybe the conversation would have been far too emotional for those people, to visualise what would have happened if we had made a different choice. Maybe the other options with this pregnancy were just too horrific. But I needed to talk through the choices, imagine the other outcomes and understand the logic and the emotions that bought us to the decision that we made.

I was able to have a direct conversation with the counsellor at Edward's Trust. I was able to express how I felt, with no interruption or delay. For the very first time, someone challenged my thoughts in a productive way.

She calmly asked, *"Well, let's consider what your other options would have been."* I don't think anyone had ever said that to me, but it was what I needed.

I simply explained, *"I feel like I was his life support machine, and that I made the decision to switch that support off."*

Even during the first session, it felt like a switch had flipped in my mind. I alone had not made this decision. Highly qualified and experienced medical professionals looked at every possible diagnosis and investigated other options, before the fatal conclusion was given. So, this was the best outcome for a horrible, unforeseen situation.

I remember walking out of that office like a weight had been lifted off my shoulders. I had no choice. It was the only decision. I wasn't the person I was telling myself I was. I wasn't cruel. It was the loving choice to make. It made me realise what I could or couldn't control.

It helped me understand how important the sense of control is in my life.

The power of talking is really underplayed in the UK. Mental Health is seen as something that should be talked about in hushed tones, with sideways glances and far too much judgement. The combination of the counselling and medicine enabled me to rebuild myself; to heal mentally months after the physical remnants of the pregnancy had disappeared.

I've always been intrigued to find out what approach Edward's Trust used. The difference it made to me was life changing, but at the heart of it, it felt like a conversation. I didn't notice the "counselling" happening. There was no bright light or comfy sofa to recline on. Just two people, in a room, chatting, with a massive box of tissues for the unavoidable tears.

I thought it may be useful to find out more about the counselling methods that worked for me. So, if you like the sound of how it helped me, you can have a better idea of the theories used and use this for your counsellor search.

I was lucky enough to speak to my counsellor from Edward's Trust as part of the research for this book, and this is the insight she gave me:

> *"At Edward's Trust, we tend to follow a 'person-centred approach' when counselling a bereaved parent who has lost a baby/child. We follow 'Core Conditions' as expressed by Carl Rogers. Through this approach, we lead with the belief that the client is 'the expert in their life'. All our counsellors listen with non-judgemental empathy and understanding ensuring to mirror and track how their client is feeling in terms of their bereavement.*
>
> *In essence, our counsellors like to think they walk by their client's side whilst on that journey, expressing care, companionship and warmth at all time."*

I remembered the work of Carl Rogers from my university days. Carl Rogers was a Humanist Psychologist who believed in looking after the whole person, always concentrating on the unique perspective of the individual. He took on board the individual's subjective experience and focused on person-centric therapy.

This approach influences how the work is supported scientifically. It's not about numbers and tests in a lab, but the reality of how the theory helps people; what they report and what they experience. It's been around since the late 1940s and still makes an impact today. In fact, as we have found, this approach pretty much helped me heal myself.

And, in a lovely twist of serendipity, it's pretty much the way that this book is being written. Trust me, you know the best way to work through this loss.

NOT A TALKER?

Talking therapy isn't going to be the best fit for everyone. It worked for me, but only when I talked to the right people. You may find that you are not ready to talk. You may find that you are done talking. But this doesn't mean that you can't access support.

Some of the wonderful parents that have contributed to this book have shared what has worked for them. Let me share some of that now.

Mindfulness

This is very popular now; western society has been a little slow at keeping up with what eastern philosophy and medicine has known for a while: that not having the mental tools to cope with a stressful life can lead to physical and emotional distress. So, when we are thrown a curve ball like grief, or a difficult pregnancy, or both, it is no surprise that the associated stress and anxiety can impact our long-term mental health and wellbeing.

If you think that mindfulness is sitting on a cushion, cross legged and saying "*Om*", I'll set you straight. There is a growing body of science behind the positive impact of mindfulness. I personally love Ruby Wax's book *" A Mindfulness Guide for The Frazzled*". Ruby has a MSc in Cognitive Mindfulness, and defines it as:

> *"a way of exercising your ability to pay attention: when you can bring focus to something thoughts quieten down ... It's not about paying attention to something outside but about being able to focus inside, being able to stand back and watch your thoughts without your usual commentary on them... My definition of mindfulness is noticing your thoughts and feelings without kicking your own ass whilst you're doing it" (pg. 34 – 35).*

When we are surrounded by negative thoughts and feelings, it is easy to get overwhelmed. I have used this approach to pay attention to how I feel, accepting it as a feeling not a fact and visualising it moving on. Maybe consider finding a local class, searching out tutorials on YouTube or downloading an app; I highly recommend the *Headspace* app.

If you are being treated for depression, anxiety or post-traumatic stress, always talk to your doctor before you use any mindfulness as it's not always recommended for those that want to disconnect from clinically traumatic memories.

Artistic expression

Art and creativity have been mentioned in conversations and in the amazing baby loss stories. For some, this is drawing, for others it was writing; poetry or blogs. All of this is a way of expressing emotions without having to engage with another person or verbalise how you feel. Some people have started journaling, using a daily diary that tracks their thoughts. Automatic writing is an interesting approach, where you write in a stream of consciousness. No stopping. No editing. No judgement on sentence structure or correct grammar and spelling. Purely letting the emotions and thoughts spill out onto paper. For others, it may be more structured; maybe a blog or a book. What do you think could work for you?

Eye movement desensitization and reprocessing

Otherwise known as EMDR, this has been shown to be useful for people that have experienced trauma or are going through grief. Practitioners believe that using rapid eye movement can help the brain process upsetting memories. This is always undertaken by a professional and you don't need to speak at all about what memories you are trying to overcome. A few people have used this and found it very useful to reduce the emotional response to their trauma. If you search for EMDR, you can find local qualified therapists that use it.

Exercise

Like mindfulness, there is a growing body of evidence that exercise does our emotional well-being just as much good as our physical wellbeing. By moving, our body releases feel-good chemicals called neurotransmitters such as endorphins, serotonin, and dopamine, all of which are known to help us control our moods and uplift them. Now, I am not a natural 'mover', but I can vouch for the release it gives. On a practical level, it can reduce some of the tension that grief carries around with it. It is a great support as the results outlast the time you are moving about.

Pills

Sometimes you just need to take the drugs. To allow myself to accept the other support offered, I needed something to help me. In this case, the help came in the form of drugs that were prescribed by a doctor. Antidepressants.

Nothing to be ashamed of.

But the pills that you need may differ. It may be as simple as taking things to reduce anxiety. It may be multivitamins to make sure you are getting what you need. It may be Magnesium to help your energy or Valerian root to help you sleep. It's about finding something healthy to help your mind and body process and heal. It goes without saying, anything that should be prescribed needs to be with the support of a medical professional.

It shouldn't take something like baby loss for you to decide you are going to look after yourself. Take this as a starting point to pay more attention to what you need; not just as a healing process, but to look after yourself all the time.

You deserve it!

SIX: A FAMILY GRIEVING

"No rule book. No time frame. No judgement. Grief is an individual as a fingerprint. Do what is right for your soul"

Anon

I find it astonishing that there is such a disconnected approach to supporting those that are grieving. I think it is closely linked to the inability for some people to really comprehend that miscarriage or late loss is still death. It's not a medical process. It's not just bad luck.

The impact of the death goes way beyond the mum.

It impacts everyone who were looking forward to welcoming that little person into their lives.

When you are grieving as a family, there is the added complication of loving the very bones of the people that are grieving for the loss of their baby. It gets complicated and messy. You are trying to get your head around your feelings and answer your questions whilst protecting the feelings and emotions of those around you.

Everyone is dealing with their own shit, whilst not being quite sure how you can all help each other through it.

I know what I did, I know what I didn't do, I know what I would do differently. But the one thing I don't know is what other people went through. I can't get into their head.

Let's open the conversation right here and start talking about how it impacts everyone. Dads, partners, siblings, and grandparents.

WHAT ABOUT THE SIBLINGS?

Out of all the things that I wish I could change about what happened, it would be that our little girl was exposed to a horrible truth about pregnancy. At the tiny age of four years old she became aware that a pregnancy doesn't always lead to a baby.

She has only recently learned about the first miscarriage we had; at a time in her life that we felt she had the emotional maturity and the biological understanding to deal with it. I think it may have been around the time she had "the talk" at Primary School.

The one thing I was worried about was how this experience affected her. On the morning of our twenty-week scan, we had told her that we were going to find out if she was having a baby brother or sister. She had been desperate to be an older sister since she could talk. She was so excited!

She had already seen the DVD from the private scan we had when I was nearly fourteen-weeks pregnant. Something so precious to us now, that digital recording of when he was kicking around, moving and tumbling in my stomach. The only time we saw him moving.

We had left her at my parents when we had the scan. On the way back from the hospital, after hearing about how poorly our baby was, I told Scott that I couldn't be the one to tell her. He took her into the garden and told her the baby in my belly was poorly and we wouldn't be bringing it home (at the time we didn't know we were having a boy). I sat, trying to explain through tears to my parents what was happening.

We *had* to tell her, there was no choice. But the conversation didn't end there. We had to answer her numerous questions. However difficult it felt at the time, in retrospect, it really helped. Trying to explain this all to an inquisitive four-year-old, simplifying chromosomal abnormalities so she would understand, meant we had no choice but to process it.

So much of the support that is out there focuses on mum, from getting her through the birth to accessing bereavement support. What I didn't consider was how it impacts the children that are already around.

At the time I was gaining some support from SANDs, via their Facebook Group, and a book called *We Were Going to Have a Baby but had an Angel Instead* was recommended. It arrived within a day of the online order, and I sat down to read it with her. I thought it would explain what happened in a way she would understand. What I hadn't bargained for was how longstanding the impact of her brother's loss would be on her behaviour and outlook on life. When she started school, she would talk about her little brother. He would appear on family trees and paintings. The teachers knew what had happened, so there was no surprise when I didn't turn up with her brother in my arms at the school gates. What I noticed was she associated all her sad feelings with the loss. She seemed to believe that his death was temporary. That one day, they would meet again.

After speaking to the teacher, I referred Grace to Edward's Trust so that she could have bereavement support. Once a week for eight weeks I dropped her off and waited whilst she spent some time with her counsellor. To this day, I am not sure what was said in the room. All I know is that she got closure, and that is the most important thing.

Hindsight is a great thing. When I look back, I wish that we had accessed support for her earlier. We would have changed the way we talked to her about the loss. I maybe would have been there, with her dad, to tell her what had happened.

However, this part of this story is not mine. It is hers. I am so proud of the strong person that she has developed into and wanted her to share her views on the loss and what helped her:

> *"Isn't it weird how when a child or a teenager gets an illness they are such a brave person, but when it's a baby, it's such a brave family. I don't think that is right. Callum Wilcox is my brother whether he lives with me or not. Obviously, losing a baby is a horrible thing, and no-one wishes it for themselves or their family, but it has made our family stronger in a strange way.*
>
> *I've had to deal with death from a young age, I think I now understand it more than other people, as I've become more empathetic. A lot of families don't have something sad in their lives to come back from. I am really proud how we haven't let it control our life. We learned how to enjoy ourselves again. For other people it has happened to, we can share our experience.*
>
> *Before I went to Edward's Trust I would never really talk about him. If I ever got sad, I would bury it down inside of me and try and forget about it. Edward's Trust taught me that I can't just forget, it's a massive part of my life and I need to face that. One of the memories was a book called "Bag of Worries". It was about a girl who carried around a big bag of worries (they looked a* bit

like germs) Every time she got worried about something she would stuff it into her bag, and that way (she thought) she would forget about it. Everywhere she went, she would carry about this bag with her and every day it weighed her down. She thought if she unzipped the bag, the worries would upset everyone around her, so she just carried it around with her. One day, she met this girl who convinced her to let all her worries go, and when she did, she felt as light as air. This story really helped me talk about my feelings and when I started talking to my parents about it, I understood it so much more.

One of the things a child needs to hear is "you can talk about it". Although, it is really hard when you are pressured to talk about it and trying to get your head around it. So, let your child come around in their own time.

Trying to explain to a four-year old that the baby she was excited for isn't coming home with us after all is a hard thing to say. I suppose what I needed, and what I got, was the hard, cold facts. Not just a wishy-washy "he's in a better place".

So, I think parents should always give their children the facts about loss, but if they are a younger child, then simplify it for them. Also, if they have never experienced loss before, you should explain in the best way possible – you know your child best.

A lot of people at my age (or younger) experience death through grandparents or animals. I didn't really get the whole illness thing. I hadn't thought that you could die when you were young. It confused me a bit, I grew up a lot. I think I got "death" better than other people in my class.

When I think about it now, I didn't really realise how rare it was. Now, looking back, it was crazy it happened to us. I know it happens to other people in the world, but not us.

The thing is, though, I don't really remember much about when it happened. I don't really remember my Mum being pregnant with him. I don't even remember being told he was poorly. I just remember the feelings. I remember more about my little sister being born. I can't remember thinking about it with Lily or being scared it would happen again. I always just assumed that things were different this time round. I think it's good, it means it didn't traumatise me.

When I found out more about it, Potter's Syndrome that is, I didn't like to hear the word. It took on a new meaning. I remember, in Primary school, we were doing a project on Egyptians and their art. The Teacher asked us to decide on which table would do "Potters" and who would do Jewellery. The word made me feel sick, and I said I couldn't do it. One of my friends knew what had happened, and what the word meant to me, and helped me move tables. At the time, the word sounded evil – now I know it's just a name for an illness.

What advice would I give to children that are going through the same thing? There is life on the other side of it. You will get through it. It is a big thing, and I went through this stage where I couldn't understand why we (me and my family) were so upset, we haven't even met him. And then I realised whilst we have not met him, we had him in mind, excited for a life that we were going to have with my little brother. He was growing inside of my Mum for five months – I realised he was a person in our head. We expected what he was going to be like. I would have someone to play with. It all collapsed.

My last thoughts? It is a terribly sad thing but isn't going to change your life or who you are. It may upset you, but it is normal to feel upset. You feel upset when someone dies, you are going miss them because you love them. And when a baby dies, they ARE that person, and they are someone you are going to miss. Never for a second think it is your fault. It is not your fault. And it's not your parents' fault. It's no one's fault. Nothing caused it. It's just one of those things in life that happens!

Life does go on, eventually."

At the time of writing, we are eight years on from her brother's loss. She is now in secondary school, and is a positive, grounded and empathetic, young woman.

I hope that by sharing her views on a really distressing time in our lives, as much as it has changed me and her Dad, it has become a part of her outlook on life. The memories that I have of that time and the worries that I had, have gone, as a lot of what I remember has not stuck around for her. The moments of crisis and concern that are etched into my brain, have disappeared for her.

So, what have I learnt from talking to her?

Be a role model

What has happened, has happened to you all as a family. You might feel like you are protecting your children, especially with a miscarriage, but our children pick up on our grieving through our emotional behaviour. This is a perfect opportunity to show our children how to deal with such a life changing situation. Become their grief role model. Show it's healthy to talk about it, make sure nothing is taboo, and encourage them to talk about how it affects them.

Consider their emotional maturity

We only told Grace about our earlier miscarriage recently, as we felt like she has the emotional maturity to deal with it and had covered the technical stuff at school. At the time we had told her that I had a tummy ache, which made her feel a bit sad. With the loss of her brother, we made sure we explained what had happened in a way that she would understand.

Children are a lot more resilient than we give them credit for

When I asked Grace to contribute to this book, I was a little worried about what I would uncover. I sat her down and explained that I wanted everything she felt – good and bad – and waited for a revelation. What I ended up with was a picture of child that has grieved but is still resilient and reflective. Whilst I would do everything to have protected her from this, the fact is I couldn't, so we made sure we dealt with it as a family.

Be sure about how you want to express your beliefs about death

If you have a religious or spiritual belief system, wonderful, but be prepared to have this challenged. Don't force it on them. Quite often we have blind faith about how we see the world (and this includes atheists too), so allow your children to ask the questions they need to ask, even if it doesn't mesh with your belief system. It is OK to answer, "I just don't know."

WHAT ABOUT THE PARTNERS?

Dads and partners seem to be ignored a lot in the process of parenting. For my husband, after the back-slapping congratulations for a positive pregnancy test, he was pretty much ignored. Yes, he came to the scans (and thank you to whomever I need to thank that he did – I can't imagine how it must be for anyone to learn what we did on their own), but apart from that it was about me. It does such an injustice to dads and partners. They are just as invested in the bundle of joy as the mums are.

So, when things go wrong, when we discover that we won't be bringing that much-loved baby home, where is the support for the partners?

I have a very vivid memory of walking in the local park next to our house, not long after we lost our little boy. We are lucky enough to live next to a nature reserve, and I always find a bit of greenery and physical activity lifts my mood.

We decided to get ourselves lost (and genuinely did – Google maps was needed to find our way home) and I asked my other half if he wanted to have any grief counselling. I was still accessing it through the hospital at the time.

His answer?

"I'll sort myself out when you are OK."

I answered, honestly, *"I'll never be OK. Don't wait for that, it's not going to happen the way you expect."*

This is one of things that I bang on about a lot. Where is the support for the supporters? There are partners who are grieving whilst supporting partners that are not only going through the physical loss, but the emotional one too.

No matter how hard I try I can't delve too deep into his head, so I have turned over this part of the book to him.

> *Whenever I meet new people, or get to know acquaintances a little better, the conversation naturally comes around to family. A six-and-a-half-year age gap generally raises a question and I have become more comfortable discussing the facts; that we have had four pregnancies but only two children. The first pregnancy was as text book as pregnancies can be: painful, draining, restless and that was just me. We were new parents, and everything changed; the way you look at everything, the way you think about everything, the decisions you make all change for the better.*
>
> *Time came to try for number two, success was swiftly followed by sorrow. We found out at the first scan there was no heartbeat. This was devastating, but very common, we were told. We left a waiting room full of life, filled with parents in various stages of pregnancy; we left the next room feeling totally alone. We were now members of a club we didn't know existed, we soon found out we already knew some existing members. Close friends and family had all either been affected directly or knew of people who had been. This was new information, I wasn't sure what to do with. Should it help me accept what has happened? Should I forget the previous excitement and anticipation I had been feeling? I just didn't know.*
>
> *It was so very different when we had Callum. We were looked after so well by the doctors and midwives. We*

were treated with care, we were not given false hope but facts. We were referred to a specialist sonographer to ensure no errors had been made during the previous scans. We were given the information we needed in a manner and tone we understood. We were well informed, supported and not rushed or coerced in to any decision. We were told to take our time and given the facts, for me this was very important and fundamental in our survival and subsequent courage to try again.

When we delivered we were left to bond, the room was ours for as long as we needed. Our baby boy was named, washed, dressed and photographed just like every baby born should be. I didn't appreciate or realise the significance of this until a long time after. The midwives looking after us knew what we needed and provided it, which was so important. I often think of them and how much they gave us that day. It really was the foundation of our recovery and I will never forget it.

Back home to reality, we had a young daughter who was oblivious to our grief and who needed her parents to continue being her parents. That's what we did. The few people who were aware were informed and the sympathy came along with the comparisons of similar tales. They didn't come with competition but with understanding. One or two said the wrong thing, but the close people, the ones that really count said little but offered everything.

I look back, and I didn't seek out any help or assistance. I informed my manager of the situation and that I would be unavailable until further notice. I was lucky enough to be working in an experienced team that could cope with my absence at short notice. When I returned, my manager asked for a meeting with me to see how I was, he asked if there was anything he or the company could do for me. He also insisted that the time away from work would not be taken from my annual holiday allowance and would be paid in full. Something I hadn't even considered. I did feel supported and cared for.

No one really said the wrong thing to me, although I would hear about the few that did to Clara. It was the usual "It's for the best" line that is such a throw away comment and so pathetic it might as well be replaced by blowing a raspberry.

Friends and family listened and offered help, but when this happens to you, there is no quick check on the "to do" list and start distributing tasks. It's as if you are waiting for someone to say, "hang on we made a mistake, everything is going to be ok". But slowly, very slowly, you start to realise this is happening and it's not going away. No one can go through it for you, but many special people made sure we didn't go through it alone, which was awesome. One very close friend of ours jumped in her car, drove one hundred miles and turned up with shopping. I believe she apologised for not being able to do anything but just being there face to face for the day was a massive gesture and really helped.

The things that have helped me heal is time, family and friends. I've learned that I can face anything, if you can find strength and purpose in a situation like this, if you can still be there for your family and not shut down and isolate yourself, you can face anything.

Now, when changes come up, I am practical; analyse it, discuss it and get on with it. To be honest, that was my approach before. What is different, now, is the realisation that nothing is taken for granted, nothing lasts forever, and change is constant.

As we travel through life we collect scars, some will be enjoyed and worn like trophies, others will never truly be cherished but shouldn't be hidden too far away. They are just as important as the positives as they define us and make us who we are. There are many cute phrases about life's ups and downs but ultimately life does go on with or without you. It's OK to check out and take yourself away for a while, but whatever network you have and rely on also relies on you. You are in control of you and how you feel and react to the world around you. Try to add fuel to the emotions you most want to feel, and never give up.

For the dads and partners going through this now, consider this:

Take as much time as you need, but keep people informed

If you are employed be honest and tell your line manager what is going on. Even if they do not, or cannot, support you they must be informed. Don't set yourself any targets about recovery time, because you won't achieve them.

Do not blame anyone, if your situation isn't due to any mistakes or negligence

You will feel all the emotions and feelings you have already experienced so far in life: happy, sad, tired, etc. but also numb which may be a new one to you. I remember thinking I should be feeling more than I did but I believe this was shock. I thought shock was supposed to feel like a surprise, not necessarily a nice one but an instant all-encompassing emotion, not this cold, detached, lonely feeling. There is no script or formula for coping or recovering but talking to people and asking for help is vital.

Remember that grief is worn differently on all of us, some of us don't show it at all

So, talk, even if you think you can't talk. People are amazing and capable of more than you think. Especially in adversity, anyone that cares about you will want to fix you, they will realise they can't but will offer all they have to you. Lean on them and take what you need because one day you may be needed to give it back. Time is not a great healer, people are. When you are ready, talk.

WHAT ABOUT THE OTHER FAMILY MEMBERS?

I never thought I would have to bury my child. It's unnatural. Having to consider funerals and coffins and readings before their life had even started. Having family around me helped support us, not just on a practical

level (school runs and childcare), but by having someone to chat to. However, I will be honest. I hadn't really considered, until I started this book, how it must be for a parent who is grieving for a grandchild whilst watching *their* child grieve.
Again, like so many conversations about this type of bereavement we are confronting head on, right here, together, I want to take some time to consider how it must be for the family that has another layer to their grief. To be watching their children going through a painful and devastating time, whilst carrying their own grief with them.

I asked my Mum to give me her views on things. Because, to be honest, this is the first time I've asked, *"How was it for you?"*

> *Clara, my daughter, was happy, safe and in a secure marriage when they had Grace, my first grandchild. I have never known the happiness and wonderful feeling that overwhelmed me to have a grandchild. Just as powerful when Clara was born. Love holds no bounds especially when she is your own flesh and blood.*
>
> *Having miscarried at nine weeks, Clara fell pregnant with Callum in between moving houses. The old saying of "New House- New Baby" certainly seemed to come true. Grace was so excited at becoming a sister and we were all looking forward to the birth.*
>
> *Tragically at five months the saddest news that ever came from Clara's lips, that the baby could not survive as it had no working kidneys. Clara appeared calm and accepting of what was going to happen. Tears flowed but, on the surface, she was pragmatic about the situation. I was listening and trying to find the right words to say.*
>
> *What do you say to your own child who is going to lose a much-wanted baby?*
>
> *How do I stop crying and put aside the sadness I felt about losing a much-wanted grandchild?*

No one prepares you for these situations unless you have been through it or experienced someone close to you. I had neither; I have never known anyone who lost a baby and my own two pregnancies were straightforward and uneventful. I had no knowledge or experience to draw on. Because of that mistakes were made on my part; saying the wrong things or not saying the right things. There are no guidelines for this.

I looked after Grace while Clara and Scott went into hospital to give birth to their baby. I was awake all night worried and upset thinking what she had to go through to give birth to a baby they would never take home. I hadn't heard by the morning, so I phoned the hospital and was informed that they had a baby boy born sleeping. Emotionally I was a wreck but had to put that to one side as we had Grace who was only four years old. I desperately wanted to be with Clara, just to hold her, just to protect her. That was Scott's role now. As a mother I just wanted to take away all the sadness and as a grandmother I wanted the baby born; hoping that the scans were all wrong and that Callum would be ok.

How do you help your child who is in so much emotional pain, hormones raging through her body and no child after giving birth? I always thought, "thank goodness they have Grace," but that does not help. The loss of a child is immeasurable.

I felt helpless and hopeless. A double whammy seeing your own child in such a state and losing an already loved grandson.

I was working at the time and had colleagues that I could talk with, only then did so many stories of stillbirths and miscarriages came out. I then realised there are so many women who are suffering in silence, even grandparents. Until something like this happens no one mentions baby loss. It's hidden.

Have I changed personally since this? "Yes" is the short answer. I will never ask a couple when they are going to have a baby. I will always be excited about mothers and their pregnancies, but I know I will be secretly hoping and wishing that all will be well. I now have much more empathy for mothers and fathers who lose a child. The trauma and deep sadness do not go away but does fade after time.

My biggest problem and always will be finding the right words when you too are grieving.

What would I say to someone in the same situation? Stop being the parent, or grandparent, trying to put things right. Be a friend, a shoulder to cry on, listen, be angry at the world together. You cannot put things right, but you can only be there for support and love. Do not be judgemental, do not compare. In turn you will need all these things from your own friends as the grieving process and loss is twofold.

DON'T TAKE IT PERSONALLY, NO ONE KNOWS WHAT TO SAY

The topic of miscarriage is still such a taboo. It has moved on a million miles from our parents' or grandparents' generation, where there would be cover ups, secrets and silent grieving. Now they have names and we have blogs, books, groups, films, fundraisers and, most importantly, funerals.

Despite all of this, it still gets brushed under the carpet. We expect that people live a full and purposeful existence and pass away, with a lifetime full of memories left behind them. But when it's a child who hasn't even taken a breath, it is a concept that many people cannot begin to comprehend.

The one thing that I noticed through our loss was how it impacted the people around me. When I lost baby number one, and especially when I lost Callum, I felt like a pariah, as if sharing this experience with people that hadn't had a loss I was tainting their life. It was as if I would somehow project our bad luck onto them.

I know, it is ridiculous. But it appears I wasn't the only one to think this way.

When we started telling people about what had happened with our little boy's development, and what it meant for us as a family, people fell into one of two distinct camps. A helper or a wrong-footer.

The helpers

Messages such as *"What can we do?" "How can we help?"* and *"I am so sorry".*

These were few and far between but meant more than I can explain. I always remember one of my best friends, who packed her car to the brim with several days' worth of delicious food, then drove three hours up the motorway and sat with me whilst I spoke, cried, drank tea, and cried some more. She was with me the day that my husband went back to work. One of the first days I had been on my own for weeks. She wanted to make sure I ate and that I had company. Even to this day, I cannot express how much that mean to me.

So, I say it here, in print, *"Thank you, Lucy."*

The wrong-footers

I won't lie. This is the part of the experience that I have carried the most anger about. Even as I write this, I can feel the bubble of upset in my stomach; it surprises me how raw it still feels. You may feel the same. If you do, I tell you this now. Don't be angry with them.

The people that end up saying the worst possible things, are saying it from a place of care and love. As human beings we tend to want to fix things. That combined with the culture of a very British stiff upper lip and a hesitancy towards emotional outburst, means us grieving parents can end up being at the receiving end of some of these wonderful lines:

> *"At least it happened now and not later."*
>
> *"There was obviously something wrong."*
>
> *"It just wasn't meant to be."*

"You can try again."

"At least you CAN get pregnant."

"It's God's way."

"They are in a better place."

"At least you didn't know them."

"Well, it wasn't really a baby."

"So, are you over it now?"

"Now the funeral is done, do you think you can move on now?"

"I know how you feel because I lost my dog/cat/grandma (delete where appropriate)."

"Please stop talking about it – it's making me feel uncomfortable."

"Well, you are paranoid about pregnancy now."

"At least you can have a drink now."

Or, the harsh one. Simply saying nothing; radio silence.

Above are some of the ways that I, and other bereaved parents have been "comforted" over the years. The reason for including this list is to show how common these "foot in the mouth" reactions are. People just don't know how to talk about it.

Before this happened to me, I fear I may have said something that may have landed painfully, regardless of if I meant well. I can't guarantee that I won't do it again, even with what I know now.

The best advice I can give you is what I tell myself. For the people that stuck around, and said the wrong thing, they tried. But they were there. Forgive them.

For those that didn't stick around and didn't say anything at all, they may have been struggling with their own life challenges and knew they couldn't support you the way you needed. Forgive them.

Life is genuinely too short to be angry. Turn that energy into sharing what people need to hear. Share your story so that people know it's not a taboo.

> *"The act of forgiveness takes place in our own mind. It really has nothing to do with the other person"*
>
> *Louise Hay*

SEVEN: TIME TO SAY GOODBYE TO GRIEF

"You will find that is necessary to let things go; simply for the reason that they are heavy"

Unknown

There will come a time in your life that you will realise you need to stop grieving the life you would have had if your baby had come home with you.

You need to start living the life you have, and start facing the reality of what is happening right now I spent far, far too long pining for what we had lost, living a life half lived, always comparing to what would have happened. We already had one child, but I remember finding spending time with her painful as she reminded me of what I had lost. I cringe and feel so sad writing this now.

I would compare reality with an imagined future, and the reality would always come up short. I would feel frustrated and disappointed and helpless. It was only a matter of months, but I think of all that time that I wasted not paying attention to the life I had.

I remember viewing the house that we live in now, when we were house hunting. It was before I got pregnant with him. We were hanging around in the spare room, wondering and worrying if it was big enough. I recall saying how silly it was we were worrying about the bedroom for a child that didn't exist.

I think this shows the power of imagination – the way we could clearly see the life before it happened. The conversations turned to plans. Those plans became purchases, and then we started calling that bedroom the baby's room.

The moment that things started to change for me was gradual and gentle. Nothing big and dramatic. It is only when I look back that I can really connect the dots.

You may be reading this, waiting for the great tipping point, the plot twist. I may disappoint you there.

It's hard to know what happened first. It might have been deciding I wanted to feel better, when I started making new plans, or maybe the fact that I started to feel better meant I wanted to. What I do know is that my behaviour changed. I started accepting and committing to this new version of my life.

The practical, pragmatic and logical side of me told me to get real and live more in the moment. I needed to take my life off pause.

To be blunt, there were the things I could do now I was a parent to a school aged child and not a new-born. I remember having a bit of an internal battle with humyself; not really knowing what to do when living with grief.

You may hate me for being so direct. But I won't apologise for saying it, I told you I was going to tell you the truth.

Dependent on where you are in life, this attitude may feel very raw. This is not to insult the memory of our loved ones or belittle what has happened.

This is me, writing eight years on.

2010 Clara would probably tell modern day Clara to jog on.

But, I say this with love.

Your life can't go on pause. You must start living again.

You can't be defined by what you have lost.

You can't be defined by who you have lost.

You must live for the people that are in your life, right now. For me, it was my little girl (and partner in crime), Grace, Scott, and my family and friends.

It meant saying, "why the fuck not?" when an opportunity to audition for some vintage promotional work came up. Just imagine, a thirty-something mum ending up becoming the face of a makeup range!

It was thinking, "why the fuck not?" when a new job opportunity came up. It catapulted me in to a whole new career path and led me to self-employment.

It was saying, "fuck yeah!" to some wonderful holidays, to home improvements and quite fabulous times out with friends.

Let's get one thing straight. There is not one millisecond that I don't wish that my babies were here. There is nothing about my experience that I consider a trade-off.

Very simply these were the cards my life has been dealt. And I'm going to play them to the very best of my ability.

I don't have a religious bone in my body. As far as I'm concerned, we have one life to live as well as we possibly can. We owe it to ourselves and those left behind to do so.

And do you know what. When I got that urge to have fun again, to have genuine, belly-laugh, fun; to seek out new things, to live as much in the moment, I knew I was starting to heal.

There was one big clue that I was on my way to happiness again. That was that I felt absolutely no guilt that I was happy.

Not one iota.

I didn't feel the need to justify what I was doing, to play it down or apologise.

So, test it out now, what would you like to do, to bring some joy back into your life?

There is a great psychological concept that you may have heard of, called "Fake it 'til you make it". As it is written about so well in Richard Wiseman's Book, *The As If Principle*, if you behave in a certain way, eventually you will change how you feel. Take smiling for example. Let's try it now.

Force a smile. Really hard. Longer than it is comfortable.

OK, if you are on bus, this has got a tad awkward.

How do you feel now?

More uplifted? More relaxed?

Happier?

Here comes the science bit … the 'smiling' muscles in your face have been activated and have sent messages to your brain to tell it you are smiling. Therefore, the associated feelings attached to smiling have been generated, flooding your body with feel-good hormones.

Isn't the human brain a wonderful thing?

That is a very simple exercise but gives you a clear example of how making small, regular changes in how you behave can change how you think. And then how you think can change how you feel. And how you feel changes the way you behave and, well, I think you get the rest!

FUNERALS AND MEMORIALS

Like any bereavement, having a way to say goodbye to your baby is important. It helps you mark what has happened so that you can move forward. Not move on, but just put one foot in front of the other. How you do that is up to you. I've heard from some parents who simply said goodbye as they walked away from the scanning department, but others, like us, had a funeral and a place to visit.

For our first miscarriage we wanted a way to remember, but one that was just for us. I've discovered I have a few sentimental bones in my body. I wanted something that would create a legacy, so we planted a gorgeous tree in our garden. It blooms every year.

But when we had our little boy, the situation was so very different. He had a name. A weight. A date that he arrived in the world. We had memories. We needed to do something more.

The hospital was great, offering support and connections; they introduced us to the most amazing Humanist Celebrant. She turned up, a glorious, tattooed, sports car driving oracle, and was the first person that spoke to us in her no-nonsense way that I came to love.

Funerals are such strange things. I can probably count on one hand how many I've been to in my thirty-something years. They are desperately sad, but also create moments of joy - retelling stories and sharing memories.

But I wasn't sure how to prepare for burying our little boy.

I think the preparation for the funeral was the first time the power of words really hit me. I spent many a night going through my musical playlist and many a search engine to find something that could sum up what we felt.

Then, I came across the words from one of my musical guilty pleasures. The country and western legend, Garth Brooks. (I grew up in a household of very eclectic music. It wasn't unusual to hear U2, Cliff Richard and Kenny Rogers in one day.)

The chorus of *The Dance* pretty much summed up how we felt. However short his time with us was, however cruel it felt to have the diagnosis, we are so happy that we didn't know what was coming when we got our positive pregnancy test. We had nearly six-months of a nervous but joyful pregnancy.

I wasn't the only one that found solace in words. Years before I found a way of writing about what was happening, Scott, Callum's Dad, wrote to his little boy and shared it with us in the chapel. I'll never get over the image of him carrying the little, white coffin up the crematorium aisle. And the way he just about held it together through the service and read it out. But it was part of his healing process, something he felt compelled to do.

Why did we do all this? It was important for us to be doing things. I think it helped us feel like we were still caring for our little boy, closing off a chapter in our lives and recognising what he meant to us.

Callum's ashes were sprinkled at the crematorium, right on the same spot that my Grandparents, his Great-Grandparents, were scattered. It is a beautiful place; by water and grass and spring flowers. A place that I thought I would want to go all the time and remember him. We did go visit, but only for the first two years. After that, it felt pointless. He isn't there and there are many more practical, useful things we can do in his memory.

So now we, donate money to Edward's Trust on the anniversary of his birth and donate toys at Christmas for children who are the age he should be.

But whenever you find us driving past the entrance to the Crematorium, he'll get a kiss blown in his direction. That is all we need to acknowledge his existence.

Our thoughts on saying goodbye:

Say goodbye however you want

We avoid religious references to our losses; but that is our beliefs. You do you. We found the Humanist approach suited what we needed when we lost our little boy. For the first miscarriage, it was simply planting a tree. Whilst getting ideas from others can be a great focus, do what works for you and your family.

Find a way of sharing how you feel

It may be using the words of others or writing what you didn't get a chance to say. This may be something you share, or you create in private. This is not just about saying goodbye, but a proven way of managing your emotions and helping you maintain your mental well-being.

Honour their memory how you want

If that is a grave, do it. If it's a starting charity to help others, do It. If it's a tattoo, do it. If it's nothing at all, then do it!

You may find what works for you one year may change the next. We started having a small "ritual" for the anniversary of our little boy's birth, buying a single white rose and placing it on "his spot" at the crematorium. But after a couple of years we felt like it wasn't right for us, so we stopped. Simple. You can change your mind and find what works for you.

Don't wait for permission

At the end of the day, this is about saying goodbye in a way that gives you comfort. Don't wait for someone to tell you what happens next. Don't wait for approval or instruction. Do what feels right.

Avoid staying angry

Anger is a natural part of grief, it's a natural part of change, but we must remember that it is temporary. There are occasions where you have someone to be angry at. Make that a proactive and positive action. What can you learn? How can you prevent things? But sometimes there is nothing anyone can do. Don't turn this anger on yourself or each other. Trust me, it's a destructive road to start walking down.

EIGHT: RETURNING TO WORK AS A BEREAVED PARENT

"I am not what happened to me. I am what I choose to become"

Carl Jung

I was treated with respect on my return to work. I went back a couple of weeks before my little boy's funeral on a phased return; Monday to Friday, but shorter days. I had underestimated how exhausted I was, physically and emotionally, so their flexibility and understanding were appreciated.

I did have the opportunity to be signed off for longer if I needed it; you may decide that you need more time. Go and speak to someone at work, someone in Human Resources or a trusted colleague, to make sure you get what you need.

Whilst I relished the idea of being back to work, doing something I knew I did well with people I loved spending time with, the return was a lot harder than I expected. My brain was still foggy with the emotional turmoil. I found it hard to concentrate. My perspective on life and my priorities had shifted beyond recognition.

At the time I was running a small team on a project that was supporting businesses to find students and graduates for work experience. I loved what I did, but when I went back I found myself quickly feeling quite angry and frustrated. It was hard to provide great customer service when you are thinking "*So What*?" when they're grumbling about candidate shortlists.

I had an honest conversation with my manager about needing to take a step back and focus on numbers instead of people. I ended up moving into a data driven, insular role. Ironically, the role that I was craving was one that I had rejected when I was pregnant as it was, I quote, *"not for me!"*. I was given the opportunity to change my role to be less client-facing, to hunker down behind the scenes. I had temporarily lost my ability to think on my feet. I had lost the trust in my emotions.

I felt like I was losing myself, little by little.

Going back to work gave me the routine and sense of normalcy that I thought I needed at the time. Sometimes I do wonder if I went back too early. I ended up having another rebound week off, the week we had Callum's funeral. The experience brought me right back to a place of emotional turmoil and I needed that extra week to take a step back and refocus.

Looking back, I do think being at home for longer, for me, would have done more harm than good. There were glimmers, even in the early days of going back to work, where I would have moments where I was just me, and not a bereaved parent.

No awkward pauses when someone saw me.

No sympathetic head nods.

Just me, doing my job.

These moments were fleeting, though. In the long run, work alone wasn't enough to help me heal, but it was a great distraction.

HOW TO ASK FOR WHAT YOU WANT

The preparation for going back to work starts within. You need to understand what you need and when you need it. When you are ready, it can be useful to regain control of the situation by making it clear what you need and asking for it.

It can be hard; I write this from the perspective of a bereaved parent who was working in a department filled with care, concern and open lines of communication. I just hope that this is something you have within your organisation or sector.

If you are finding it hard to know what you want, don't worry. Things will change over time. Just take it a step at a time and don't put too much pressure on yourself.

The first step is just to think about what you need. Before you return, consider this:

What do you want to say?

You can decide how much or how little you want to detail about your loss. If you even want to mention it at all. Let your Manager and/or HR Department know what you want to say and make it clear how you want to handle your return. Think about who you are happy to talk about it to. Be aware this may change over time. That is OK.

How will you communicate?

I made the decision to be proactive with my colleagues before I returned (the joy of remote access emails). For me it was important to have a gentle return. So, like any modern worker, I sent a group email to the people that I had decided I wanted to share more information with.

It went something like this:

> *"Thank you so much for all of your support over the past month. As you can imagine it's been really hard for us all, losing our little boy the way we did. Whilst I am back, please feel free to ask me anything you wish. Please don't walk on egg shells around me. It is upsetting, but you know me, I'm a talker.*
>
> *I'm not OK, not by a long way, but I will be, with time."*

When I left my job in 2015, I found that email when I was clearing out my correspondence. It made me smile as I remembered, how it helped me take that first step back into our new normal. By taking control of what I said to who, it meant that I was over the hardest part of any bereavement; talking about the loss on the first meeting since it happened.

What do you need?

Unsurprisingly, I was still having weekly grief counselling through the hospital when I went back. I was upfront about needing time off during the work day to attend. I tried to have the appointments as late as I could in the day; partly so I could have the bulk of my work day done, but also for my own well-being. It meant I had an evening to recoup before I was back at work.

What other responsibilities do you have?

This is both in work and outside of work. Who else can offer you support? Are there things that you could do with stepping away from in the short term? Consider all the things you must do, and truly ask yourself how you feel about them. If they are causing distress or stress, take a step back.

Make self-care a priority

Pay close attention to yourself. It's very easy to let simple things like eating and sleeping slide. Consider what energises or distracts you – make sure you work these things into your day.

UNSURE HOW TO APPROACH YOUR EMPLOYER? USE MY WORDS TO HELP

The first time I wrote about returning to work as a bereaved parent was on my blog. I remember being sat at my desk in January 2016, less than six years after it happened. I had this title echoing around my head; *A tender word and empathy: Supporting bereaved parents back to work* and felt compelled to write something. You could say this is when the idea for this book was conceived. A catalyst to start talking about loss in a way that it needed to be discussed.

The anxiety I felt when I pressed publish was palpable, it was pending for a few weeks before I felt ready. But the response to the piece was overwhelming, and it made me realise that there are so many people and organisations stuck when it comes to supporting bereaved parents. They know their bereavement processes but the discomfort surrounding baby loss and miscarriage can lead to an awkward mishandling of such a delicate and sensitive time.

The article was written as a way of reaching out to employers to get them to see past their policies and procedures, and to consider the people that this has happened to. A way to have them consider how they can make the return to work as smooth and sympathetic as possible, one to pass on if you feel it's needed.

First published 25th January 2016

A Tender Word and Empathy: Supporting Bereaved Parents Back to Work

I can't discuss supporting parents back to work without touching on bereaved parents. With an estimated twenty-five percent of pregnancies ending by miscarriage or late loss, and sixteen stillbirths or neonatal deaths a day, unfortunately this is likely to be one of the most regular bereavements staff may experience.

I am writing this post from the position of a parent that has lost two babies in pregnancy: one early and one later, and my return to work on each occasion were very different. The first, shrouded in self-imposed secrecy and the second open and transparent (as the pregnancy was obvious and public). However, on both occasions the emotional distress was the same, impacted by the physical symptoms and aftermath of the loss.

Once a parent goes through this type of loss, the stories flow; you join this strange secret club, that is never mentioned until you have experienced the same thing. As part of this discussion, I have found out how varied and inconsistent the treatment is of women when the unthinkable happens. Whilst there seems to be policies and procedures for a range of return to work situations, too often they go to the wayside in the circumstances of baby loss.

It is not uncommon to hear things like:

"I was pressured to come back; it wasn't just a feeling, but a request of a return date within days of my miscarriage"

"No one asked me what I wanted to say; when I came back colleagues asked me how my bad back was."

"I was asked how the baby was when I returned from my maternity leave: no one had said I had lost him"

Are you as shocked and upset as I am reading this? I hope so. Just put yourself in the shoes of these grieving women.

Baby loss, at any stage of pregnancy, is devastating – there is nothing a company or colleague can do to "fix it", but some simple steps can be put in place to cushion the return to work.

Ask

Very simply, ask the question *"What do you want me to tell people?"*. Firstly, when the individual contacts you about their loss, and secondly, when they are due to return. Some may want to keep it private, which is fine, but they will tell you the reason (if any) they want to give for their time away. For me, that was my choice for my early loss. For the later one, I not only wanted people to know, I wanted to talk about him and what happened when I returned. You cannot make the decision for your staff member.

No pressure

The physical symptoms and recovery from a loss vary; it is not something that is over in a couple of days. Regardless of the gestation, there is a chance some type of surgery is involved; even a general anaesthetic. Don't compare other people in similar circumstances or have the expectation that the individual will be back within a couple of days.

Staged return

When the person is ready to come back, propose the option for a steady and gradual return. Maybe shorter days? Also, consider temporary change in their responsibilities. Someone who has been off with a broken leg, for example, may get a change in their role – working from home or lighter duties. Consider a similar approach for a grieving parent. For my late loss, my duties changed to enable me to be less client-facing and more focused on detail. I needed that at the time; it didn't last forever but it meant I could still feel productive and purposeful whilst working through my grief.

Grief is real

Regardless of the stage of the loss, the grief that is felt is real. Allow the same time and sensitivity for the process that you would allow for a colleague that had lost another family member.

Words hurt

There is nothing that you can say that will make someone feel better: avoid phrases like *"Better now than later", "At least you have a child", "When will you try again?"* or "*They are in heaven now*". A simple *"I'm so sorry* "and "*How are you*?" are enough.

Future pregnancies

It is inevitable that any pregnancy after loss is tainted; extra anxiety and possibly additional midwife and doctors' appointments. I know that mine were. Future pregnancies don't magically erase the experience of the miscarriage, and often can bring back feelings of grief or even guilt. Keep an extra special eye on your colleagues at this time; take them for a cuppa as they just might need a chat.

Partners

This is my final point, as I hope that through this article you have been asking *"What about the partner?"* When a pregnancy is lost, often only the mother is thought about. Remember the dads and partners that work with you. They are not just off work to support their partner, they grieve and hurt too. The emotional impact may be different, but it is still as strong. Consider all these points when it happens to them too.

These seven very simple things, which come from a place of care and communication, can make or break a grieving parent's return to work. Just a tender word and a little bit of empathy goes a long, long way.

NINE: PREGNANCY AFTER LOSS

"Emotions are data, they are not directives"

Susan David

Like so many families that go through a loss, there is a time where life returns to as close to something that looks like normal as possible. Six months passed following my depression diagnosis and I felt solid enough to apply for a promotion at work and was over the moon when I got it. I came off my medication and conversations of trying again came up. Far too many people feel that the answer to child loss is to just try again. That somehow getting pregnant will fill the gap created by the miscarriage. This is a common solution to many well-meaning friends - *"you can just try again."*

At the end of the day, I didn't want another baby. I wanted my baby boy.

What people often fail to see is the fear created when a pregnancy is lost. The first time I felt this fear was with Callum's pregnancy, the year after our first miscarriage. I was in total denial and refused to take a pregnancy test for nearly eight weeks. I was waiting for something bad to happen, not realising what was on the horizon.

After two losses in as many years, one where I had to give birth to a perfectly formed little person, I was stuck in the middle. Exceptionally fearful, but desperately wanting to become a mother again.

The fear wasn't just of losing another baby, but fear of losing myself. I had a range of questions in my head. The biggest one:

"Could I cope with the same happening again?"

When you are fearful, you are often gripped with a sense of dread; I had lost my sense of security, removed any certainties about anything in my life, let alone the ability to birth a healthy child.

"Would I become broken past the point of repair?"

I was legitimately concerned about my mental health if the same thing happened again. But I knew what support would work for me and where to get it, which was reassuring.

We didn't even know why this had happened.

I wanted statistics. I wanted to know the likelihood of this happening again. I wanted to make sure there wasn't an insidious genetic mutation waiting to bite us in the arse.

The need for answers was the drive to make sure that we said yes to as many tests as possible. Over the months since Callum passed, we had bloods taken, tests, scans, medical records pulled and many, many probes and pokes, just to see if they could find a reason.

Others may not understand why you need answers; but if, like me, you like to see things through to a conclusion, this is what you need.

For others, you may want to draw a line and walk away.

Either of these options are your choice. I fully respect your right to choose.

The only thing I want to leave you with is this:

At some time, maybe sometime soon, our willingness to have our medical history pulled apart, turned upside down and inside out, will play its part in making a medical discovery. Potentially, a discovery that will avoid a family going through what we have gone through.

We may never get the answers we need but, one day, it may uncover something rather spectacular for others.

In the aftermath of our two losses, but centred around the loss of our little boy, we had to battle through genetic testing. Potter's Syndrome, was, and still is, a very rare disorder. The type that our little boy had (bilateral renal agenesis) where neither of his kidneys developed properly, only happens in approximately one in ten thousand births. Because of this, it was important to uncover what may have caused his issues. It was also important to understand if there were any hidden, underlying health issues for our first born and anything that could affect any future children.

The hospital appointments continued, and I carried on researching.

If your loss has any type of syndrome attached to it, it is likely you will be asked to take part in genetic testing. For us, that involved kidney scans, blood tests, hearing tests and lots of questions about our families' medical history.

At the time, it did add to our worries. *What if other things were found? What if nothing was found?* At the time, I wasn't sure what I wanted the outcome to be.

You may wonder how I managed during this process? This may be relevant to you now.

One simple way. And don't shoot me if you don't like this "G" word:

Gratitude

Yes, that seems a bit strange, considering the context. I wasn't grateful that this happened. Not in a million years.

But I reminded myself how lucky we were that the NHS existed. That, at no extra cost to us (apart from our time and few parking charges), we had thorough examinations and investigations. Through my research I had connected with a couple of other Potter's parents from the USA, who didn't have as much investigation as we did. It really felt like no stone was left unturned and I ended up getting a pretty good health check too.

I was impatient – the answers didn't come quickly enough for me. But reminding myself it was a process that had a lot of unknowns certainly made it a lot easier. It also helped us feel a little more settled when pregnancy number four arrived.

DECIDING TO TRY AGAIN

In my work as a coach, I talk about comfort zones a lot. That place where you move into discomfort, but not quite into the panic mode. For a long time, the thought of getting pregnant again placed me firmly into my panic mode. I had spent time thinking about what the risks were of trying again and playing the options through in my mind (thanks to the tools the Edward's Trust therapist had given me). Once I started thinking of the other options, I realised what my greater fear was, and I noticed a shift.

The fear of it (losing a baby) happening again was overcome by another fear; what if we wait so long that the option of another child is taken away from us?

By this time, I was thirty-two; my two previous pregnancies were spread out over two years, so I felt like I was running out of time. I was aware of my biological clock ticking away, not to mention our secondary fertility issues, so, the pressure was on. Not the best way to start trying for a baby.

This was one of my first signs that I was starting to heal. That I had the physical and, more importantly, the mental strength to take a risk.

Because, let's be honest, pregnancy, once you have had a loss, feels like a risk.

But you know what? Everything else pales into insignificance when you realise it's a risk worth taking.

Less than two months later I was pregnant.

It was a tad unexpected.

The sign? After a weekend away at a rustic Welsh castle-turned-hotel, drinking mead and being entertained by a rather hilarious jester, I woke up the next day far too hungover for the amount I drank. That combined with horrific period pains, yet no Aunt Flo, made me take a test.

In typical fashion, the announcement wasn't Instagram-ready. I peed on a stick whilst the husband was at Football practice and Grace was in bed. Then I paced the floor for what felt like three years 'til he came back from his evening out and I shoved the test in his face.

As you can imagine we were very excited but nervous at the same time. That BFP after a baby loss just doesn't feel the same. And that's OK. When you've experienced what we have, it's no surprise that one of the first things you feel is apprehension.

This is why you must start rallying your troops around you as soon as you can. These are the people that you trust, that can help physically and mentally support you over the coming months.

This is why, I believe, the Bullshit Twelve-Week Rule needs to be dropped; to be repealed.

Whoever your circle of trust is, tell them, as soon as you can, not when society deems it suitable. It's a bumpy ride, pregnancy after loss, and you will need them.

A RAINBOW BABY

> *"A 'rainbow baby' is a baby that is born following a miscarriage, stillbirth, neonatal death or infant loss. In the real world, a beautiful and bright rainbow follows a storm and gives hope of things getting better. The rainbow is more appreciated having just experienced the storm in comparison."*
>
> *Kicks Count*

I struggle with the term 'Rainbow Baby'. On one hand, I love the image of joy and the hope that it gives. What a beautiful vision, of a rainbow after a storm.

But we didn't want any further children to be defined by the loss. It would feel like they were only there because their sibling didn't make it. They wouldn't have their own identity.

When our final child, Lily, arrived kicking and screaming into the world, her very astute big sister asked, *"Would Lily be here if Callum had survived?"*

It was such a hard one to answer, but we made sure we answered it. It may be a question that you will have to answer one day so I'm giving you fair warning, so it doesn't come as a shock like it did for us.

I have reflected on this a lot and have come to a solid conclusion. I am not spiritual at all. It offers me no hope or relief. But when it comes to the babies we have lost and the ones we have, I firmly believe this:

Lily was the child I was meant to have. The previous bodies of the babies weren't well; they were broken. So, she is not a rainbow. She has not come after these babies, she has come after the experiences. She was always meant to be here with us.

This is something that her sister likes to hear, and one day, I am sure I will speak to Lily about it too.

MENTAL HEALTH IN PREGNANCY

There is a delicate nature to pregnancy after loss, and as I look back now, I realised I should have taken full advantage of the mental health midwife I was offered. Nearly ten months of underlying worry and concern should never be handled on its own.

It was only when my Manager pointed out to me that I was off sick, feeling nauseous, in the run up to each prenatal medical appointment, that I noticed how this was affecting me. The delicate balance between staying in the present and working through the past wasn't always working. The return to the hospital where it all happened, with some of the same staff, was certainly a trigger for anxiety – but it wasn't something I had recognised until it was pointed out to me.

To manage this, I investigated hypnobirthing; not so much for the birth (I'm a "*chuck as much pain relief at me*" type of gal!) but for the fear release aspect. I couldn't spend the next six months living on the edge. I had started developing nightmares and health anxieties that if left unchecked could have spiralled out of control. I started to fear going to the toilet in the anticipation of what I might find and was neurotically checking the size of my bump.

I'm a scientist at heart and have always had my doubts about anything that is a tad on the "woo-woo" scale (if you haven't heard that phrase before, it means "*Relating to or holding unconventional beliefs regarded as having little or no scientific basis, especially those relating to spirituality, mysticism, or alternative medicine").* However, one of the areas of my Psychology degree that always stuck out for me was the pain-relieving power of hypnosis, something that has historically been thrown in the woo-woo pile.

You see, even with my scepticism, I am aware how powerful the brain can be and how little we know about it. I managed my fears the wrong way in the past and I wanted to make sure it didn't tarnish this pregnancy.

The fear release treatment I had during the hypnobirthing session felt surprisingly like the release I had the year before with the counselling. Expressing the pent up anxieties I had about the pregnancy, and about me, helped me understand what was in my control and what wasn't. If you haven't already guessed, control is quite a dominant trait within my personality. Pregnancy and childbirth are probably two of the most human functions that you have the least control over. Realising this was quite life altering.

The tools and techniques given to us during that session continued throughout the pregnancy and before I knew it, May 2012 came along, and my maternity leave started. Being away from the pressures of work and having time to reflect was a real tonic. For the first time in a long time I felt like I would be bringing our baby home. I had avoided so much just in case; buying clothes, unpacking what we had saved from Grace's baby days, decorating the nursery. Nothing had stung more than having to take things back to the shops when our boy didn't make it home.

THAT'S A NEW THING. AFFIRMATIONS

Until that point in my life, I hadn't really felt the need to lean on affirmations. I always felt like they existed in the same space as crystals, Tarot cards and astrology. Please don't shout at me if they are your thing. They just weren't for me.

I understand the power of Mindfulness, Neuropsychology and Cognitive Behavioural Therapy (CBT), so when I found myself saying the same thing to everyone I told about the pregnancy, I decided it was my affirmation.

To say I was scared was an understatement, but I decided at that point to repeat an affirmation to myself and to anyone else that would be interested as a way of support.

"I will enjoy this pregnancy for as long as it lasts."

This wasn't a flippant thing. It was a crutch to keep me stable and secure for the duration of the pregnancy.

After our earlier loss, and so that people could understand what I was going through, I only told a few people (our support troupe) that I was pregnant. It wasn't a stand-on-the-rooftop-and-shout-it-out announcement like our first; we still wanted to keep the news to ourselves. Not for the Bullshit Twelve-Week Rule, but because it was our news and we enjoyed it being just amongst us for a while.

There are still little behaviour changes that come up when you are pregnant, so the eagle-eyed people noticed them. The ongoing issues with milky tea started early, and whenever we went out with work, I would look at the menu in advance to just check what I could to eat.

These affirmations popped up again when I discovered hypnobirthing. Every night, I would go to sleep listening to a relaxation track, and then, when me and Scott could stay serious for more than five minutes, we would go through the hypnobirthing script to help me focus and connect with what was going on.

Words have great power; it was amazing how rephrasing certain words, such as calling contractions, surges, would reduce my stress and anxiety considerably. It helped me through my pregnancy, eased me through my labour and then kept me calm and attentive (well as attentive as any women during the delivery of their baby!) when our bundle of joy got into a bit of difficulty making her way into the world.

I can sit here and wax lyrical about the power of hypnobirthing but wanted to share with you why it works.

After the tragedy of losing a baby, many women and their partners are understandably nervous about trying for another baby and becoming pregnant again. Pregnancy is a time of uncertainty which can be difficult to manage for any woman or couple, but even more so following baby loss. After experiencing loss, it might be very difficult for you and your partner to allow yourself to think about getting to the point of childbirth, and so you may not have given much thought to birthing techniques such as hypnobirthing. But learning about hypnobirthing may be useful in helping you to manage some of the anxiety and worry around preparing for birth.

> *Hypnobirthing has seen a huge increase in popularity in recent years and there are many different approaches, but the core ideas involve using relaxation, breathing techniques, self-hypnosis and positive affirmations to prepare for and manage your experience of childbirth.*

It is nothing like "stage hypnosis" and will never involve making you feel out of control; indeed, the core philosophy of hypnobirthing is to help women feel more in control of their birthing experience. Women often report that using hypnobirthing helps them to feel more informed about birth, more confident about making decisions, and more able to manage stress and anxiety levels.

It is important to stress that hypnobirthing should not be about pressurising women into giving birth in a particular way (i.e. "naturally", without medical intervention, without other forms of pain relief, etc.) and is not a guarantee of "pain-free" childbirth. Any class / practitioner / book / video that claims otherwise should be avoided. Rather, it is about finding ways to help you relax enough and feel empowered enough to make the right decisions for you, your body and your baby. There are different ways to access hypnobirthing, such as books and videos, online classes, group classes (private and NHS in some areas) or private one-to-one sessions with a hypnobirthing practitioner, so you can make a choice about which method of learning feels most comfortable for you and your partner. If it feels okay to do so, it would be helpful to mention that you have had an experience of baby loss to your hypnobirthing practitioner so that they can think about any appropriate adjustments to their course material and be sensitive to your needs.

Chloe Thompson-Booth: Perinatal Clinical Psychologist: Do It Like A Mother

HOW TO ASK FOR SUPPORT

There was one thing that came to light quite rapidly during my final pregnancy. There isn't really a consistent emotional support system for people who have a pregnancy after a second trimester loss.

I was under Consultant Care due to my pregnancy history, and a big part of this was due to the fact we hadn't been signed off from the genetics team at the time! I was assigned a mental health midwife during my booking in appointment. Well, when I say 'assigned', I mean I was told I could access one. I never met them (or if I did, they didn't make themselves known).

There was nothing on my notes about our previous loss. Due to the gestation of our little boy, even though *we* class him as stillborn, the medical profession does not. For parents that have had third trimester losses, it is common practise for single tear drop sticker to be placed on the notes when a mother goes in for her scans. I didn't have one of those as it happened in the second trimester.

Our twelve-week scan for pregnancy number four was the same place where, less than eighteen months before, we had found out about the fate our little boy. Whilst the room itself wasn't the same, it brought back memories and I had a panic attack. When the sonographer started scanning, my vision had blurred so much, I was convinced that there was no heartbeat. I couldn't even hear it when she turned the sound up. This emotional outburst seemed to come as a surprise to her.

I felt like there was a check box exercise going on during the whole process. This is one of the reasons why I am writing this book. A place where we can share the realities of the journey of loss.

Please don't misunderstand me, I appreciate how underfunded and stretched the NHS is. They have a lot to manage and not a lot of time or resources to do it. My community midwives were great, one in particular had been around at the time of my loss and knew my history. But, as I have come to learn from speaking to other bereaved parents, support differs.

I gained my support in two surprising places. One, from the reflexologist I regularly visited at work. She was the one, with her magic fingers, that revealed I was further ahead in the pregnancy than I believed to be (confirmed at my dating scan) and she calmly listened to my worries and concerns for the entire pregnancy.

Just spending that time, thirty minutes once a week, relaxed, attentive to what was going on in my body, and sharing my thoughts with someone who wasn't emotionally attached to me, who just listened, made such a difference.

People often devalue the power of talking. Whilst working with professionals is essential for many, many people (hell, I've been there, got the t-shirt), talking to absolutely anyone is also a great release.

I found that many of my friends would take my concerns with a pinch of salt (as apparently, *"I was now paranoid about pregnancy"),* or they were exceptionally supportive and would do everything they could to make me feel better and reassure me (along the lines of "*don't think like that*"). However, what I have learnt about myself through this process is I just need to talk and get all the bad and complicated and difficult thoughts out of my head. I don't need someone to fix it. I don't need sympathy. I just need to reduce the power of these thoughts by speaking them out loud.

So, I turned to strangers on an online forum. Hidden behind made-up screen names, we had a couple of things in common. Similar due dates and a history of baby loss. There I shared my concerns and my obsessive symptom checking.

There isn't enough credit given to online platforms. Social Media is given a bad rap. What it can offer is a way to connect with people thousands of miles away that are sharing the same experiences as you. Parents, just like us, that have lost a child and, however hard they try, those that haven't had this loss won't understand that another pregnancy doesn't wipe away the fear.

I managed to find a few other parents who had been through what we had been through. In our private, smaller groups, we shared research findings and gained hope from others that had had further babies with no complications.

We had a scan at sixteen weeks with the same consultant that diagnosed Callum's Potter's Syndrome. We turned up at the appointed time and she was in her work suit. Last time, the sense of panic and urgency was exaggerated by her wearing surgical scrubs. To this day I wondered what she was off to do after our meeting. Would it be a happy ending for another family?

Even though we were in the same room that the crushing news was given, this time there was a sense of hope. Immediately we could see that the news may be better; instead of the snow storm interference of the past scan, we saw the outline of a baby, kicking and twisting about! Thankfully the first thing she checked were the kidneys; we could immediately rule out Potter's Syndrome. Next, in what felt like a lifetime, she worked her way through the remainder of the checks, each time setting our concerns aside by reassuring what she could see was as expected. Finally, with a massive smile on her face, she told us we were having a healthy baby girl.

TEN: RETURNING TO WORK WITH A RAINBOW BABY

> *"On particularly rough days, when I'm sure I can't possibly endure, I like to remind myself that my track record of getting through bad days so far is 100% ... and that's pretty good"*
>
> *Anon*

Having such a long-winded journey to baby number two meant that I was able to save up a bit of cash to help plug the financial gap for my eventual maternity leave. This maternity leave was four years in the making.

I was watched closely by the Health Visitor Team in the early days of having Lily, due to my mental health history. I was even warned that returning to work could be a trigger for post-natal depression. It was something I hadn't considered and hadn't heard of before.

I remember my return to work meeting with my Manager, letting her know that whilst I didn't want to come back to work (something that surprised me and her), that "*this was the place I want to be*". I had shocked myself by how much I had enjoyed being off; it was over a year thanks to a generous maternity leave policy and a little bit of annual leave.

On reflection, my return to work was anxiety-ridden and if I could do things again, I would change them. I hadn't really paid close enough attention to the Heath Visitor and I had a limited understanding of what post-natal mental health could look like. I had my own experience of depression and assumed that it would feel the same; I also assumed that my depression was only triggered by grief.

I was so wrong.

Below is part of a blog I penned for *The Motherload*, reflecting on my return to work after having Lily. You may notice yourself in this:

Sometimes clarity comes with time. When you are in the depths of returning to work, balancing the delicate mixture of excitement, anxiety, self-doubt and the glee of having a cup of hot tea, and having a wee in peace, you can't always identify the reasoning for your feelings.

For me, I felt like I was grieving when I went back to work. I would have a little cry on my way into work; I would have a little cry in the toilets during my lunch hour and I would have a little weep in the car on the way back. It was crying daily, irrational fears about what may happen when I was away from my little girl.

I was in a constant state of anxiety; unbreakable nervous energy when I was at work and feeling sick to my stomach when I was at home. I started making poor work decisions in a last grab attempt to feel in control. At the time I thought that this was linked to going back to work after a year off. That it was because she was my last child – my final baby. For a short while, I believed it was because I had lost the ability to do my job well.

However, the one thing I didn't realise was this: not only was she was my last baby, she was also the first baby I had brought home since 2006. The six-and a half year age gap was not by design or choice.

There is a level of fear that underpins the return to work of a parent that has lost the naivety of life after these types of struggles. After battling through turmoil and settling into a routine that finally trusts the new family dynamic, it is all changed again with the return to work. We can't be there to make sure they are safe, that they are happy. The grief of this temporary separation is overwhelming and can come out in a variety of ways – so please don't judge yourself if you end up being panic stricken with red-rimmed eyes when your mobile rings.

This may sound familiar to you. The job that you lived for and the goals that you were working towards, may all pale into insignificance. That isn't a reflection on you, it is a reflection on how your life has changed. It doesn't mean you don't care or that you are broken beyond repair. Just that your life has changed in a way that will take some time to re-calibrate.

When you go back to work after leave, there are some key things that will help your return be a little more positive:

Talk

Keep talking to someone you trust. This may be through a formal network such as SANDS or a trusted friend. Don't bottle up what you are feeling; there is nothing to be ashamed of! Without a doubt, if you feel like things are too overwhelming, or any negative or stressful thoughts are entering your head, speak to a medical professional to get the support you need.

Strength

You will uncover a level of strength you never knew you had. You may not feel it now, but so many of the women that I heard from in the process of this book reflect on the strength they now have. Use this to refocus what you want and take the leap to make it happen!

Purpose

Pain moves us. Pushes us out of the norm. Own it. After any transition or trauma, people get clarity on what they want. You may find that you start to want different things. It could be a new career, relationships, skills or personal goals.

Guilt

Try and move away from the guilt that you MAY feel as life goes on. Life, if handled the wrong way, can carry a level of guilt that can paralyse. Don't feel guilty for enjoying it.

Joy

Grab the joy in the little moments, as over time, those are the ones that will count! They will build and become easier to accept into the day to day and are a great antidote to working parent guilt.

CHANGE: EXPECT IT, IT'S NORMAL

Now, let's talk about some practical things about pregnancy. It doesn't matter if you have one or twenty-one, there are some things we need to discuss to make sure your return to work goes the way you want. In my day job I help parents with their work-life balance and returning to work, and I want to share with you some top tips to make your return as positive as possible. These are things that anyone returning to work should consider. Often, people that have had a turbulent journey to parenthood have so much emotional stuff to process, that the more practical things don't get discussed.

So, let's discuss them now!

The change in mind-set starts from the second you know you are pregnant; or even before. Another big shift occurs when you are returning to work. The feelings you will work through are big, and they may trigger the underlying emotions that are left over from your loss. Understand these feelings are normal and are not a reflection of your commitment or capability.

Respect the emotions you are feeling and talk. Talk to colleagues and friends, local parenting groups, online support groups and other parents at your workplace. Identify the areas that are causing you concern and start researching. Be in control.

You will want and need time to settle back in

The impact of the return to work can reach far wider than the first few weeks. The practical elements of your return (such as getting back into your computer!) are not the only thing that should be considered.

Give yourself a "maternity return induction" to settle back in; reconnect with your team, department and your colleagues. Don't expect to sit down and just pick up where you left off. Reflect on when you had your last holiday. I expect you had updates with the team, caught up with emails and read meeting minutes. Maternity leave is time away – regardless of the reason – by no means is it a holiday, but the concept is the same. No question is a stupid question, get the clarity that you need to feel informed.

Don't make assumptions about yourself or each other

The version of you that's returning is a different person to the 'you' that left. What you want out of your career and personal development may have changed.

If you've come back on a different working pattern, don't be apologetic about it. Be clear about working patterns and your availability through your email sign off and face to face updates.

Verbalise and set your career goals with your manager

Don't wait until your annual review or appraisal to set goals; get these in place as soon as you can when you return. It will provide you with focus and direction. Make it clear to your manager and colleagues (and yourself) what you want career-wise and how you will achieve it.

Be open and honest about what is achievable within the hours that you work; don't put unnecessary pressure on yourself if you have moved to a part-time role or you can't be as flexible with working overtime. Consider what you have learnt about yourself in the time you have been away and be clear about what you need to do your job. This could be simply refreshing your IT skills or to improve your confidence in public speaking. The skills you have are still there, just a bit rusty!

Parental Leave: Start the discussions early

The earlier the better for this point. Ideally, before you go on maternity leave. Get your hands on the company policies including Keep in Touch Days (KIT) and Flexible Working Requests. Understand them and how they apply to your individual circumstances.

If you are looking to change your hours via a Flexible Working Request, make sure you have a compromise position and ideally speak to your manager before you return. Remember, it's a two-way discussion process. If a decision can't be made on the outset suggest a trial process, maybe using any accrued holiday you have. During this, you could uncover and make recommendations around efficiencies or process changes.

Remember your Keep in Touch days. I personally regret not taking mine. I thought I wouldn't want to know too much and that I would end up mithering. I can see now that they were a great chance to stagger the return to work and get up to speed with colleagues and the job without it impacting on maternity leave. It also gives a financial boost at the end of the unpaid leave period.

Communication

Share experiences and perspectives, and connect with colleagues who you feel you can confide in. Engage with the mentor programme or a coach if you don't have a sympathetic or supportive ear.

If you only remember one thing from this section, remember that consistent communication with friends, family, your managers and your colleagues will help you have a positive return to work.

ELEVEN: THE BABIES THAT COME AFTERWARDS

> *"You know, they say the cracks are where the light gets in, but I really think the cracks are where your light gets out. Yeah, the beauty you don't realise you have. The strength inside you never get to see. The bravely you demonstrate by showing up every day, by trying, but not giving up ... It's in your cracks that we see your light. And you're bright, darling. In your deepest, darkest days, you're just so bright."*
>
> *S.C. Lourie*

She arrived on a rainy June day, screaming in frustration to a room full of nurses and doctors, then proceeded to show her affection for her dad by emptying her bowels all over him! The relief was immense, especially as she had decided to get stuck on the way out and had turned a relaxed and gentle birth into a room full of stony-faced medical professionals. Her cuddly ten-and-a-half-pound frame had to be temporarily swaddled in a blanket as her new born clothes didn't fit. After overnight observations we were told we could go home. I sat and waited for her to meet her big sister. In a world of social media and camera phones, we had decided our new-born needed to meet her big sister before she made her way into the online and real world of our friends and family.

There is something you don't realise as a grieving parent, and that is how much our other children absorb and take on board. Whilst I had spent time in treatment, and my husband and I had taken the time to keep up a positive but realistic approach to this pregnancy, our then-six-year-old had been silently assessing the situation.

As she sat beaming, holding her sister for the first time, she turned her head to me and asked, "*Are we really bringing her home? She isn't going to die?*"

At that moment we realised how we'd all been holding our breath for that moment. That for nine months, we had been secretly asking ourselves this question. Not until that point could I confidently answer, *"yes, she is coming home with us."*

PARENTING AFTER LOSS

I was really worried I would turn into one of those dreaded helicopter parents once Lily arrived. You know the ones, metaphorically wrapping junior in cotton wool. I was so determined to get to the end of the pregnancy with a healthy baby, I hadn't given much thought to how I would feel once she arrived.

When you have lost the way we have, you have a new sense of fear; you know what it feels like to be out of control and the grief that follows. It is no surprise that your parenting style may change following that. Whatever experiences we have leads to a change, but you have the added fact that the world of parenthood has moved on. When I looked at the difference in advice in between my pregnancies, and in between the birth of my girls, it is no surprise we get confused.

I had such a different approach to weaning, sleeping, feeding, and only some of it was influenced by what happened. The world of parenting had changed in the six-and-a-half years since I held our first new-born.

It is important to recognise that how you feel about children will change when you have a loss. Whether you have children already, or have children after, you have a layer of apprehension or fear that might not have existed before. You must follow your instincts as much as possible, but also take time to reflect on your approach. It can be easy to live life in fear, to restrict what you do with your kids, or what they do without you as they get older because of anxiety.

The best way to manage this? Pay close attention to your decision-making processes. Why are you saying yes to what you say yes to, and no to what you say no to?

Be realistic and understand what a genuine risk is and what is influenced by your fear creeping in.

What can you do to minimise the feelings of concern that you have? How do you normally build trust in yourself and other people?

You ask for help. Share how you are feeling, be it with other parents or family members. If you find that this fear is having a negative effect on your day to day life, reach out. Anxiety can be a sign of post-natal depression, so pay attention to your own wellbeing.

HOW TO EXPLAIN THE ONES THAT CAME BEFORE HER

At the time of writing this, my youngest daughter is six years old. She is our last baby, the one that arrived after all the heartache and worry.

I won't lie, I'm not sure if she knows about her brother. Whilst we do have pictures of him, they are in a subtle cubby in our lounge, so I don't know if she has noticed. She has never asked about who the baby is. It is something that I battle with - how to bring it up. How to explain. She is a very different child to her older sister who was born with a very old head on young shoulders. Lily lives in the moment, is obsessed with dinosaurs and cars and transformers; she lives in a world of adventures and goodies and baddies.

Whenever his name comes up in conversation, as it often does, I mention he is the baby that lived in my belly before her, and he was too poorly to come home. She looks at me, a little blankly, and then carries on saving the universe! This may be an acceptance of the fact. It may be a lack of connection. I imagine we will only uncover this as she gets older.

To clarify, what I am saying is that this is something we have yet to face. She hasn't asked about this baby. She hasn't requested a detailed explanation of what we mean, or who Callum is. She hasn't questioned anything, yet.

But we're determined to not hide anything from her. We want to be honest and answer any questions she may have, whenever they arise.

It may confuse her. It may upset her. It may not affect her at all. We can only do what we can to help her process it.

There is only one point that we must hammer home. She mustn't doubt, even for a second, her place in our family.

My greatest fear is that she will feel like a replacement or second best to the babies who came before her.

Think about how you would describe it to the children that come afterwards; maybe one of your children was very small when the loss occurred. Start thinking now how you would like to talk to them about it and prepare yourself before it happens. It will be emotional. You can do it, but it helps to be prepared so it doesn't come out of the blue and you end up handling it with a knee jerk reaction.

HOW A HASHTAG WILL FINISH OFF A CHAPTER

Sometimes, life comes together in a unique way. One of the joys of working for myself is the opportunity to write more. Like many others, I discovered the joy of blogging. I was drawn to write an article on how my grief has changed my life, entitled *Strength after Sadness* that was published on *The Motherload.*

My writing for *The Motherload* was the first time I had shared what I had experienced with our losses openly; previously it was a practical, advice-filled blog on my business website. The words flowed so easily, like they do now. I think it was finally time for me to share what we had been through.

Once the piece was published, like all good bloggers, I started with my social media sharing. The response was amazing, with lots of support and stories being shared. But I didn't see what happened next coming at all.

I went onto my Twitter account to share it, and, out of curiosity, entered #PottersSyndrome in my search bar. With a tap of a key, my life would change once again.

There, within the references to Harry Potter, was a news article about a baby girl in America. A baby girl with Potter's Syndrome who had survived! In 2013, a little girl was born to American Senator Jaime Herrera Beutler. She was three months premature, weighing just 2 pounds and 2 ounces, and had what our little boy had, Bilateral Renal Agenesis, which means she had no working kidneys. But, on this occasion, they had used a revolutionary treatment to inject saline into her mother's womb, which replaced the missing amniotic fluid that causes all the problems with Potter's Syndrome. That was enough to strengthen the baby's lungs enough to be given a chance.

I have kept a quiet eye on this family, and found out that the little girl, Abigail, was successfully given a kidney transplant (from her Dad) in 2016, after spending the first two years of her life on daily dialysis.

I won't lie. When I set eyes on that first article, I felt sick. My stomach dropped to the floor. "*How is this possible? What did we miss? Could have Callum survived? Did we make a mistake?*" But as I read on, it became clear. This baby girl is the first to have survived a new and revolutionary treatment that enabled her lungs to develop enough to allow her to survive outside of the womb, and then have a kidney transplant when the time was right.

No amount of money or time would have made any difference to our little boy.

But maybe, just maybe, his medical results have fed into that treatment and one day, in the future, no family will have to go through what we did. Maybe that feeling I have, right now, *that* is post-traumatic growth.

TWELVE: DON'T FIGHT THE NEW NORMAL

> *"BREATHE. You are doing fine. Sometimes fine is wonderful. Sometimes fine is brave. Sometimes fine is Okay. Sometimes fine is making it. Sometimes fine is being real. You are doing fine. BREATHE"*
>
> *Rachel Marie Martin*

Whilst I was writing this book, the working title was *The Baby Loss Manual.* It sounded crass and makes me uncomfortable, even now, but I couldn't quite get this phrase out of my head. Why? Well, it was simply something that I wanted when we went through our miscarriage and late loss. I craved a step-by-step guide to help us get through it and help me understand what I was feeling, how to get to grips with the practical side, and how to speak to family, friends, work, and our little girl.

And, most importantly, how and when I was going to be in a better place.

The key thing I have come to realise over the time that has passed and through the process of writing this book, is how powerful the word OK is. In the early days, I was longing to be OK. All I wanted was to find a way of getting through the hours and days and to get back into a happy medium again.

However, there is an issue with this; the assumption that I, and we as a family, could get back to where we were before it all happened.

People talk about wanting to get back to normal. Waiting for the moment things will get back to how they were before. But do you know what? There is no back to normal.

This is your new normal.

Any life experience, good or bad, affects you. It moulds who you are as a person and changes the way you think about the world and yourself. Right now, life is likely to feel a bit discombobulated. Never heard of this word before? It means "*to confuse, disconcert, upset or frustrate.*"

It pretty much sums up how I felt in those months and years after we had our last loss. Things had started to settle, our 'official' grieving period had been and gone. I was back to work, settled, and happy.

That's right, happy. Content, even.

And all of that left me feeling discombobulated. I was confused about how I felt, frustrated about the fact we had to go through all of this. What happens is that your grief settles. It isn't at the forefront of your mind, but it will often appear from nowhere.

A smell.

A sensation.

A name (even now I struggle a little in playgrounds when I hear someone calling "*Callum*").

A scene in a TV show.

But I also had moments of complete joy, of peace and happiness and laughter.

I would talk about our little boy with a sense of nostalgia and sentimentality. I was proud of how we came together as a family. I'd watch my girl play or get absorbed into a book or film. You get the gist.

So, my message to you is this. Don't wait until things return to normal. Don't think you have to wait until you feel like your old self. Your life has changed, potentially beyond recognition. You will be trying to process what this means for you, your family, and your future. The person you were pre-baby loss doesn't exist anymore. You won't be that person again.

If you understand that positive experiences like travel, new relationships, self-development or education will change who you are as a person, then you must accept that this experience will change who you are too.

THE IMPORTANCE OF MILESTONES (AND WHEN I FORGOT ONE)

There will be a time in your life where the loss will not be the first and last thing that comes to mind. It'll naturally settle into the framework of your being – the same as any other experience in your life. It will feel strange.

You may have carried around this grief, like another layer of your being, for a while now. Feeling better may not happen straight away and there isn't one thing you need to do to start to heal, but it's likely to be a combination of different things. It's only when you look back that you can see and feel the progress, and then you notice that the feeling remains.

In the meantime, life will be carved out by a selection of milestones. The due date is the biggest one. After that, they become anniversaries.

You may decide to mark them, like how we spent Callum's due date on holiday – to quietly remember him, but have fun, too.

Then, the following year, on the anniversary of his birth, we visited and laid a white rose where his ashes were scattered. But over the years those milestones have passed in a quieter way; we've found more practical ways to mark his memory.

The milestones themselves were an indication that things were changing for me. One year I only remembered it was the anniversary of his due date on the *actual day*. I was sat at my desk, scanning my diary to book in a meeting, and noticed the date. This meant I had none of the emotional lead-up, no internal tracking of what may have happened on that day.

I'm telling you this to reassure you that there will be a time where other activities, no matter how positive or mundane, will replace the rawness of a date in a diary.

A LETTER TO MYSELF

This book is the book I needed to read when I was dealing with the way my two pregnancies ended. This is the closest I am going to get to reaching out over the years and tears and help myself move on. In the process of this, I keep writing a letter to myself, one that I wish I could deliver, to give hope and reassurance that things will be OK.

I have found writing so therapeutic, so I want to share my letter with you, in the hope that you will one day find the strength to write your own. Consider how you feel now. Write a letter to yourself, maybe one for the future or one for the past. See how it makes you feel.

"Dear Clara,

I know you won't believe me right now but trust me when I say you will feel happy again.

The pain is so raw for you right now and I know how torn you are. The wish that you can just crawl under the covers and just sleep until everything is better. The babies that you so desperately wanted, and cared for, aren't with you, but the life that has grown from the pain is so wonderful.

You are raging against the world. You haven't lost your baby. You haven't misplaced him. He was taken from you. Everything feels so unfair. I get it. I really do.

I remember the days between diagnosis and Callum's birth, you were still taking those prenatal vitamins. You were still looking after him, right until the end. Making sure everything was as gentle and kind for him as possible. But you must make sure you are just as kind to yourself.

That is what I need you to do now. To be gentle on the one person who needs it right now. Give yourself a break. You don't have to be the strong one. You don't have to always be the brave one. Even though everyone tells you, that you are. Ask for help.

I know you can't even imagine how life will be in the future. You can't think straight; your mind is foggy with emotions, confusion, and anger and such a never-ending pool of sadness.

I started this letter in the car, before book club. That's right, book club. You know, the thing you would do when you were older. Well you are doing it right now. Your life carries on in a way you can't even contemplate now. But it was only when you reached out for help. You dropped your "Teflon shield" and admitted you were struggling. You can't even imagine how many people rallied round you, the support you got, and how this pieced you back together.

The thing is this. On that day when you told Scott "I'll never be OK", you weren't lying. Life isn't the same, but in so, so many ways it's much, much richer.

You are so much more tolerant, resilient and open to experiences. You have made some big changes in your life which means that you are on a steady path, one that you can control and that is filled with wonderful people, your glorious family and so much fun.

You are, and remain to be, the parent you want to be.

So, this is what I have learnt. Be open, be honest, look after yourself and realise that your heart will heal if you ask for and accept help. Pay attention to the little wonderful things in your life, without guilt, as they will help you bring the fun-loving joker back to the surface to stay.

With love,

Clara"

SO, WHAT NOW?

The biggest, most unexpected change I experienced was how what I wanted out of life shifted. But who I am, the very core of my being, hasn't been altered too much. I'm still a feminist book-worm with a penchant for person-development books and a little too much chocolate.

But what has changed is what drives me, what I believe about myself, and how I view the world.

When you have gone through a monumental shift in your perspective, it can be hard to reconcile who you are now with who you were before. If this experience has changed your life beyond recognition, it can feel like you have lost your direction and meaning.

You may be someone that had a spiritual or religious life before this has happened, and your experience has rocked your belief system.

Rather than panic and feel rudderless, let us work together and start to redefine who you are and what you want.

We are going to work on your values.

What are values?

> *"Values are a mirror image of who we are at any moment."*
>
> *Hopson & Scally*

So, this is who you are, right now. We are coming to the end of the book, and the start of your journey to heal.

To be able to move forward (and note, this is not how to get over it) you need to get back in touch with yourself. Pregnancy, regardless of how long it lasts, means you give yourself over to another purpose. Another life suddenly takes priority over yours. What you want or what you need is second-guessed by the impact on the other life that is growing inside you.

You may have found you are now stuck in a limbo about who you are and what you want. You have had a moment where what you wanted, and the life you imagined, has been snatched away. Out of your control. If, like me, that has repercussions to your mental well-being, you may have had a longer journey back to where you are now.

You may be at the very beginning of the journey.

You may just be reading this book as you're interested in how we did it.

Either way, wherever you are in your journey, working on your values is an essential part of life.

I'm putting my coach hat firmly back on now. For you to work on you, to get clear on how you are going to move forward in your life and start focusing on what you have in your life, you need to recognise what is important to you.

Values are the driver behind our choices and behaviours. The values that we carry with us are often unconscious, but they have been created by our life experiences, what we have witnessed and the messages we have been given about success by the people that really matter to us.

What helps is coming up with a list of value words.

You need to set aside about five minutes to do this exercise. Don't spend much longer than this, as you may end up over-thinking it, but work through each of the four steps. As with anything that I suggest, it is best performed alongside a cake and a cuppa (hot drink!).

1. Mark any of the words that resonate with you. The ones that represent the values that are important to you.
2. Now, group the words together that mean the same thing, or are related to each other. Give each group a word that sums it all up.
3. Rank these groups in order of importance.
4. The number one ranked group should be the one that is most important to you. If it's not, have another look at your ranking.

Values words

Achievement	Adventure	Art	Creativity
Challenge	Community	Democracy	Honesty
Altruism	Effectiveness	Fame	Health
Independence	Family	Friendships	Growth
Nature	Recognition	Balance	Love
Loyalty	Money	Order	Pleasure
Power	Relationships	Religion	Responsibility
Security	Self-Respect	Stability	Status
Success	Time	Truth	Reward
Understanding	Connection	Wisdom	Spirituality
Cooperation	Risk-taking	Spontaneity	Awareness
Patience	Integrity	Anything else?	

What next?

Think about the values that are most important to you. How are they showing up in your life? How are they driving the choices you are making? And although it may sting, acknowledge the ones you are avoiding.

I want you to spend some time thinking of all the elements within the life that you have. The one that we have acknowledged exists now, not the one we are pining for.

Consider your definition of these values and ask yourself, how are they showing up in your life?

I'll help you by mapping out some areas:

- Relationships
- Career
- Health
- Personal growth
- Finances
- Family
- Leisure

The importance of taking control

I'm going to take you back in time, to late 1996. A classroom in rural Birmingham, and a much, much younger Clara Wilcox who is half way through her Psychology A-Level.

My amazing Teacher was going through the theories of depression and talking about the locus of control. Now, over twenty years later, this is something that has stuck with me and is the backbone of how I have lived my life.

Locus of control is a concept of how strongly people believe they have control of experiences and situations that affect their lives. Those that have an internal locus of control believe that what happens in their life is related to what they do to make it happen. They take credit for the good and bad things (within reason) that happen to them. This is me, if you hadn't already guessed.

For those that have an external locus of control, they believe that they have no control; good things happen through luck and when bad things happen it is someone else's fault.

As research has progressed, it has been found that those that have an external locus of control *("Nothing I do makes a difference*") have a higher link to stress, lower self-esteem and depression.

Before we go further, let me set something straight – this is about moving forward and taking control of how you want your life to be. It's about considering this in context of what we know we can control. What has happened to us is out of our control. Fact.

The good news is that a healthier and internal locus of control can be learned. It can be practised and then become second nature.

We are now going to think about what you can control.

What you want out of life going forward, things that cover all elements of your life and are linked to your values, right now.

This isn't about wishful thinking and *"if only*". It is about taking realistic and practical steps towards what you want to do and away from what you don't want.

If you find yourself drifting into self-blame or an internal monologue that involves expecting to control things that are very simply outside of your control, then stop. Regroup and ask yourself, "*Is this within my control?"*

One of the guaranteed ways for you to positively impact your health and well-being is by making changes and acknowledging the effort you have made and the impact you have had. Understand what you can influence or change.

When I look back, this was the tipping point for me. Realising that putting my energy into things I could influence and change, rather than fighting against the things I couldn't.

But this is a step-by-step process. Start with the small things that you want to work on. It may be something that you want to change. It may be something that you want to keep.

So, I ask you now, after looking at your list, what's the first thing that you want to work on?

SILENT COACHING

Don't worry, I haven't left you high and dry, this is the part where you start planning. Here is the worst kept secret for you; in my day job, I'm a coach and mentor. A certified coach, not a self-proclaimed one. What I want you to gain from this book, is not only a sense of hope, but also practical steps to rebuild yourself and your life.

This part of the book may be too early for you. You may come back to it in a few weeks, or a few months, but I want to make sure it is here, waiting for you when you are ready.

This is how you work out how you are going to make the next steps in your life happen.

How you are going to create a step-by-step plan to take control and make the changes you want: and need.

Considering the areas of life that you want to work on, ask, what's the one you want to start with? Grab yourself a pen and paper, and work through and ask yourself these questions:

- What will I do?
  Be SMART (*specific: measurable: achievable: realistic: timebound*).
- When will I do it?
  Not just the deadline, but when in your day and week will you carve out time to make it happen?
- How will I do it?
  Be as precise as you can to consider the steps you need to take.
- What do I need?
  What resources do you need? These could range from money, opportunity, space, connections and more!
- Who could help me?
  Do you need someone to help you? From someone that will support you, to someone that has skills or experience that you don't have.

- What may stop me? How will I recognise this is happening? What is your procrastination sign? How will you know when it is stopping you doing what you want?
- How will I over-come this?
  What will you do about the procrastination sign?
- How will I celebrate?
  The most important thing. How will you celebrate and who with?

Before we move on to the final chapter, I want you to find someone to share your plan with. Someone who knows what you are planning, who will gently support you and to check in on your progress. Who will hold you accountable? Tell them your plans – right now. Feel free to email me on hello@thebalancecollective.co.uk and let me know your plans!

AND HERE ENDS MY STORY

Here we are, at the end of this part of our journey together.

Whilst it has been cathartic for me to write, I wanted to share my version of life after loss to let you know that life will carry on.

This is what we have been through, how we have moved on, how it impacted us and the steps we took to get back on track. I wanted to share what is often unsaid and hidden to make you feel less alone and helpless.

But it wasn't just my story, I have had the privilege to share the stories of other mothers who haven't been able to take their babies home.

So, this final chapter is a roundup of what we have learnt and what worked for us.

Pick and choose what works for you and where you are in your baby loss journey.

Feel what you feel

Don't bottle up your emotions and don't let other people tell you how to feel. Find a way to express yourself, be it through talking, or another way that means you aren't getting caught on an internal loop of negative thinking. This is not just for your own good, but for the good of your relationships – friends and family, the people that will be grieving alongside you.

There is no deadline on grief

But don't let it outstay it's welcome. Don't feel like you only have a set time period to grieve. This may lead you to burying your feelings before they are ready to be processed. But likewise, don't live your life by the expectations of others. If you feel better quicker than someone else did or faster than you did before, then that is OK.

Don't make assumptions

You may find you have default set of coping mechanisms. Up until now, they have worked. These could be "keep right on", "denial", "talking", "find new things" or something else. However, just because your coping mechanism used to work, don't assume it will for this situation. It's unique. If you find it's not working, don't beat yourself up. Don't assume that you are the issue. Try something new. Maybe try the opposite of what you usually do and see what happens.

Ask for help and accept it

For me, this help ranged from medication, to therapy, to people bringing me food. This may be the hardest thing to do, especially if you don't have many people around that know about what you are going through. There is no sliding scale on who deserves help; early loss versus late loss hierarchy is bullshit, so don't get stuck in that way of thinking.

Start living again as soon as you are able

The strangest thing about my grief was the way it pressed pause on my life. I felt like I couldn't enjoy my life even when I wanted to.

Find a way to connect with what brings you light and laughter into your life.

Find the new you

Let's be blunt, loss like ours is a trauma and a change. Two things, as human beings, we don't like. We like life to be predictable and safe. When something like this happens, it shakes up the core of who we are and what we want. So, when things go back to your new normal, it's not unusual to feel discombobulated. Take time to decide on what you want now. It is not a bad thing to draw a line under your life before and start a new chapter.

Get some focus

Nothing is more motivating and re-energising than finding a new focus. Losing a baby can make you feel helpless, so regain that sense of control by finding something to work on. Find something positive that will add something to your life, or solve a problem, or give you an imaginative distraction that will energise you.

This is part of who you are

Like any experience, good or bad, it is now part of who you are. Don't assume that you can keep all the good stuff and dump all the bad – but remember that you have a choice about how it affects you. Be aware that it will leave its calling card on your psyche; for me, there are certain things I can't watch on the TV now and I react to change very, very differently than I did before. Pay attention to how this part of your life shows up in the future.

Life will go on

Usually, life goes on for others before it goes on for you. That is probably the hardest thing that I had to get over. But you can't read their minds. You have no idea about what they are feeling. Don't make assumptions based on the behaviour of others. The last thing you want to do is spend your energy on the opinions and actions of others – stick to who you can influence and those who really matter to you; starting with you.

Remember this doesn't define you

It will become part of your life story. Even part of your emotional DNA. It may lead to new things; many bereaved parents use this experience to start charities, change jobs, move to a new house and change their perspective on life. However, it is not the only thing that makes up their personality. It won't be the only thing that makes up yours. Remember who you were before. Remember who are you now. Be assured that, at some time in the future, this won't be the only thing that occupies your mind.

So, here is where I hand back over to you. Take what you have learnt from this book, find the first thing you want to do, and take the first step. Your journey will be different to mine; it will be different from the others that have contributed to this book. But it is a journey that will change you. For the better, I expect.

I leave you with some words from the creator of the Grief Curve, Elisabeth Kubler-Ross:

> *"The most beautiful people we have known are those who have known defeat, known suffering, known struggle, known loss, and found their way out of the depths. These persons have an appreciation, a sensitivity, and an understanding of life that fills them with compassion, gentleness, and a deep loving concern.*
>
> *Beautiful people do not just happen"*

OTHER JOURNEYS

> *The friend that can be silent with us in our moment of despair or confusion, who can stay with us in an hour of grief and bereavement, who can tolerate not knowing...[.] not healing, not curing ...[.] that is a friend that cares"*
>
> *Henri Nouwen*

As so many of us discover when we have lost a baby, it is something that happens more frequently than we realise. However, a silence surrounds it, especially with early loss, which means we can't always access the support when we need it. After our experience with our two pregnancies, and whilst researching this book, it has become my mission to remove the taboo from loss.

For some of the women that have contributed to this book, it is the first time that they have talked about their loss. Or the first time they have spoken about it, outside of a few, trusted people.

As we have seen, putting our pain down in words reduces the power of grief. It allows us to share our experiences. Reduce the feelings of isolation and shows the variety of ways it can impact us.

By sharing their stories, it also shows hope. Hope to move forward. Hope to regain their sense of life and joy.

So, let's say their names and not let them be forgotten.

LJ – MISSED MISCARRIAGE

Back in 2010 I had a missed miscarriage. Up until then I had never heard of it and I was shocked by the number of women that quietly said they had experienced the same loss. I was also surprised and saddened at how much this grief and loss seemed to be a big female secret; women were not discussing it until I talked about my experience. For me, talking is important to make sense of things and to help me come to terms with what is happening in my life. I found these conversations were limited and that I couldn't find support online. In the end for my own healing I started to write a private journal. The journal became my confidant. I still find it painful to read and it's tucked away.

My baby was due on the 5th November; November is the month my Father was tragically killed in a car accident when I was younger. I felt strangely confident that it was all meant to be as I couldn't have another loss in the month of November. I had convinced myself it was a girl and we would name her Poppy, so when I lost this pregnancy I felt confused, bereft and inconsolable that another tragedy would be in that dreaded miserable month.

I have never felt heartbroken before and I genuinely feel that without the support of my friends and mum I would have lost my mind. It was hard to function and lots of my friends were getting pregnant which felt bittersweet.

On my first day back at work a heavily pregnant woman came out of the lift I was waiting for. I burst into tears and literally ran away. I caught the bus and I went to Birmingham Botanical Garden. I sat there all day on my own and cried. I was inconsolable.

My husband tried to be helpful and kind, but I felt he thought I was over reacting to it all, but I loved his belief that we would have another baby, with time. That was my anchor of hope.

My son was born February 2011 and he is an only child. I always say to him that "I made a wish for you and my wish came true", but the truth is I remembered begging and praying to the universe because I would do anything to have a child. I became very single-

minded in my desire to get pregnant and looking back I think my other half was a saint to put up with my obsession.

On the 5th November I light a candle and I remember that tiny life that didn't make it; no one else remembers, but a mother always will.

I hope that now, women are more open to speak of miscarriages, still born babies and infant mortality. It's a part of life and I believe talking and sharing experiences is a great healer.

We own our bodies and we own these stories, and if it helps parents come to terms with this life experience then that can only be good thing.

AS: UNPLANNED PREGNANCY

On the 12th December 2012, I found out I was unexpectedly pregnant. I was terrified. I had just moved into a new house with my long-term boyfriend so, although relatively stable, we were not planning on having a baby. We had decided that right at the beginning of the relationship, nearly five-years before.

When I read 'pregnant' on the test I was shaking, numb and so confused. Over the next week or so after having the test from the Doctor, I started to believe it was real and as I had taken the precautions to prevent a baby then there must be some sort of fate involved.

I had accepted that my life was going to change in a monumental way.

On the 22nd December, I had a spot of blood in my underwear. There are so many articles and forums saying not to panic so I didn't. I called the Early Pregnancy Unit but due to the time of the year there were no appointments available; but I was told to go in to hospital. We went to A&E and I explained the situation and was put in a side room and given another test. After what felt like hours, but it may have only been forty-five minutes, the friendly doctor came back with a big smile on his face and said "Great news! You are pregnant. The test came back and you are five-weeks pregnant."

My heart sank. I explained that this cannot be right because I was nearly seven weeks. The doctor said to just go home and relax and to come back if there was any more bleeding, and he sent us on our way.

On the way home, I bought a pregnancy test to check my HCG levels. When the words 'not pregnant' showed up on the screen, I ran downstairs wailing. I couldn't stop shaking and telling my boyfriend that I was so sorry. I had physical pain in my chest like my heart was being ripped out. I remember vividly that as he was holding me whilst I made noises of grief that I have never made before. I kept screaming things like:

"I'm so sorry!"

"I promise I would have tried to be a good Mom, I really would have tried my hardest."

"I didn't plan for the baby, but I did want them. I would have done anything for them!"

He knew I was just venting and looked after me saying that I shouldn't be sorry. None of this was my fault and of course I would have made a good mom. He had no doubt in his mind.

I didn't bother to go back to the hospital. I just put on a sanitary towel to go to bed and overnight, just like that, my pregnancy was over. I went to work on the Monday as it was a normal working day on 24th December and explained to my boss that I would do the main bits of work but that I needed to go home early. He was amazing and told me off for even coming to work in the first place.

The next part was dealing with Christmas with my family. I had already written Christmas cards to them all from the unborn child saying things like, *"I can't wait to meet you,"* and, *"I'll come out when it's a bit warmer!"* so I had to throw those all away and tell my sisters and my father the sad news. I still felt guilty, and now I felt guilt for their loss. My boyfriend's family were so upset for me, in fact my boyfriend's sister said how awful and unfair it was and it was her worst nightmare for that to happen.

It made me realise that there were so many people around me who planned for children and got them, so maybe that's just the way the world works. This baby wasn't right for me. Who knows what caused the miscarriage? All I knew is that for the few weeks I was aware of being pregnant, I did everything by the book, including turning down the open bar for my work's Christmas party.

I called to cancel my scan and they told me to go in any way to make sure 'nothing was left behind'. After hearing horror stories about miscarriages, to be honest I felt lucky that mine was so swift, simple and physically pain free (although my heart was shattered into pieces). I can't imagine the extra emotional pain if it would have been any more than that. Although by this time I was a lot better, I did notice that I wasn't really offered anything more than a leaflet about miscarriages and I remember feeling a bit lost.

A few days later, I had a phone call on the bus home from work. It was from the local Midwife to book me in for all my appointments and checks. I had to explain to her over the phone that these were no longer necessary, and I honestly felt sorry for her. I imagine that a lack of communication means that midwives must make awful phone calls like these a lot.

On my due date my Boyfriend planned a lovely day for me, as he couldn't predict if I would be ok that day or not. This was extremely thoughtful of him and it just showed me one of the many Fatherly qualities he has. I try not to remember my due date, but I know it was mid-August, but forgetting the date has helped me heal.

If I had any advice to anyone about this, I would say *absolutely* do not blame yourself. It's inevitable that you do, the word 'miscarriage' itself made it feel like I had done something wrong, but these things are not something that can always be prevented or controlled.

I ate right, I didn't touch one drop of alcohol and have never smoked in my life. I was even avoiding smokers in the street to avoid passive smoking. I went above and beyond what I needed to do and still lost my baby. There was nothing more that I could do and blaming myself would only make the grieving worse. I can only control certain things in life, and one of them is my own reaction to life. Yes, I still feel sad about it from time to time, but instead of feeling the loss, I like to think of it as we weren't ready for each other, because in November 2014, just under two years later, I gave birth to my gorgeous healthy Daughter.

My baby came back to me.

Just because a baby is not planned, does not mean that it is not wanted. So, if anyone says to you (in an odd way to cheer you up) "Oh well, it's not like you wanted the baby anyway" or tries to dismiss or brush off your grief, then tell them to keep quiet and take a seat.

Your grieving is just as valid, and your pregnancy loss is just as important.

Do not feel guilty for mourning a baby that you did not plan for.

Life is full of surprises, good and bad, and you cannot predict or plan for it all. But you can control what you do with the experiences. I always make sure I tell any pregnant woman I know to get anything checked that they are unsure about and stay away from Google.

Go to a GP and don't worry about seeming neurotic or wasting their time, because a GP will not think that. To be honest, if I hadn't gone to the hospital when I did, it would have given me more ammunition to blame myself for not seeking medical help.

KA: INCOMPATIBLE WITH LIFE

We waited until we were buying our own home, we had travelled the world and were ready to settle down. We had savings in the bank, and everything was pointing to the fact that we were ready to become parents.

We fell pregnant within four months and were ridiculously happy. I had quit my job to start my own business. Things were going so well; baby's room painted, decorated and ready for our baby to move into. At 20 weeks, we had our ultrasound and we found out that our baby was a boy. We were over the moon, a beautiful son!

On that day, we were also told that we needed to come back because they couldn't see his heart properly. We went back two-weeks later, and the Sonographer told me that she still couldn't see the heart properly, so we needed to go to Monash Medical Centre. I knew she was lying, I could see it in her eyes. My GP later explained that it looked like there was a hole in our son's heart, but babies are often born with holes in their heart and they're fine. The equipment at Monash would be able to see what was happening and how severe the hole was. We got to Monash and after seeing our little boy on the screen again, we were told that no, he was not 'fine'. In fact, we were told, "I'm sorry, your baby is not compatible with life." The problem with our son's heart was so severe that there was no way that our baby could survive. We didn't want to believe them though, our son was so active and having a great time rolling around in my tummy, he was fine, right?!

Over the next five weeks we had test after test to see whether there was anything that we could do, each test came back with even worse news. There was nothing we could do to save our son's life, he was only alive because my body was keeping him going. We were given the option to "allow him to go peacefully", basically removing the life support system (me), or to continue with the pregnancy and lose him at any time and risk complications to me and any future pregnancies. This could also mean that we couldn't have more children down the road, which we were told that we needed to consider.

After weeks of wrestling with the decision, my son started having seizures in my tummy and then go completely still for what seemed like hours but was possibly only around thirty minutes. My whole tummy would shake and then go completely still. I rang the doctors again and asked what they thought was happening. It could have been any number of things, from issues with our son's brain to issues with his organs not functioning as they should.

We had to let him go, this was not fair on him and was just prolonging the inevitable. Our son was going to die no matter what we did. At least if we chose to, he could go peacefully to sleep and would be born with no pain, fear or suffering ahead of him. We chose that 'fate' for our son. It was not fair on him to keep him alive for our own selfish reasons. We wanted to meet him and to see him breathing, of course, but at what cost?

When we had the final ultrasound, we saw our beautiful little boy's heart, beating away with its irregular rhythm. His heart didn't form properly, there was no wall between the top two chambers and there was a hole between the bottom two chambers. The hole at the bottom was repairable, the top part was not. His organs were already starting to show signs of not functioning properly, and he had fluid surrounding his kidneys. He didn't have long left; possibly the reason for the seizures.

The only way that we could let him go peacefully was to stop his heart. The alternative was that he would die painfully in my stomach after much suffering. Or, if by some miracle he survived through the birth, he would die painfully in our arms. He would not be able to get enough air since his heart couldn't pump oxygen through his body. I could not imagine holding my child and watching him die knowing that there was nothing we could do to help him. In the absolute best-case scenario, he would live for a few minutes. Imagine the pain, fear and panic that he would feel. I could not, and would not, put my child through that.

We had the final ultrasound on the 18th October 2011. I had to lie completely still on my back with Charlie moving around in my beautiful round tummy, his head was up near my heart. At my request, I was given a dose of painkillers that would pass through to Charlie and he would not feel what was about to happen. A long needle was inserted into my stomach and then into my womb and into my son. He was given an overdose of anesthetic, so he went to sleep and never woke up. I had to lie completely still, even though every ounce of me wanted to run away and look after my son forever. I was internally screaming "NOOOOOO. They are wrong, what if they're wrong?" I wanted to curl in a ball and protect my Son from them. I wanted to kick that doctor in the throat and run away with my Son. I wanted to hurt the doctor so badly. I hated that doctor, I hated him, I fucking hated him.

I felt my son's final movements as he kicked and moved for the final time, he was surrounded by love in his final moments; his Dad, his Mum and his Nan (my Mum).

I hated the doctor, but I knew he was doing everything that he could for our Son, just as we were. He was so patient with us, he answered all our questions from the time that we first met him all of those weeks ago, right through to that final appointment. Even the repeated questions that we asked again, just in case he gave us a different answer this time. It must be an incredibly difficult job, and he did an amazing thing for us just by being patient, caring and professional. I'm pretty sure he is a parent too, so he had to separate himself as our doctor from his parent self otherwise he would have lost it and cried with us too. I wanted to hug him and punch him all at the same time.

My son was born sleeping after an incredibly painful labour. I had a reaction to the medication used to induce labour and basically had a contraction lasting for over thirty hours! The nurses would come in and top up my morphine levels when it got bad again and the pain was dulled to a bearable level. So, when labour did start in waves, it started too quickly for the epidural that I was promised; the Anesthesiologist was busy with the other women having babies that were born that night too. I wasn't prepared for labour as I was told that they would make it as painless as possible with an epidural.

We were almost 28 weeks into the pregnancy, just into the third trimester. My Son came into the world legs first, I had to push the whole time to birth him – nearly three hours of pushing. I didn't want to push, I didn't want him to come out because then we would have to say goodbye to him. The excruciating pain of pushing contractions with no medication to dull the pain, and the emotional pain of not wanting to push but also wanting the pain to stop. I didn't want to do it, I needed a break.

My Mum and Hubby were on each side of me. My Hubby was telling me how strong I was and that he was so proud of me. That made the difference, I started to push. I remember saying "Come on baby, we can do this." He was born silent in a maternity ward full of the sounds of women laboring and babies crying. We wished so hard that our beautiful little boy would just open his eyes and start crying too. Or that we would wake up from this nightmare. But neither of these things could happen.

Charlie was born on 20th October 2011, 1294g and 39cm long; big for this gestational age. He was named after his Grandfathers, two men we loved so very much. Black curly hair covered his little head, he had my chin, everything else was a miniature version of his gorgeous Daddy.

We got to hold our beautiful little boy who looked so perfect on the outside. We got to count his little fingers and his little toes, we got to give him kisses and cuddles and cry with him in our arms. We got to bond with him and we got to say goodbye. This is not how we pictured becoming parents. The pain was horrific; physically, mentally, emotionally. The doctor who gave us the needle came to visit once Charlie was born, he came to meet Charlie and to check up on us. What a beautiful person this guy is. I thanked him for everything he had done for us. The hate and anger had disappeared, replaced by respect and admiration.

We got to spend the next two- days with Charlie before we left the hospital. I gave him his first bath, then had to sit down, dizzy and overwhelmed. My hubby got him dressed in the special clothes that we bought. We got to take photos with him and my Brother got to meet him. When it was time to go home, I didn't want to take him in the car, it just didn't seem right for our son to go in the car without a proper car seat. He was transported to the Funeral Home for us. Leaving Charlie in the hospital, albeit in great hands, was awful. Leaving that hospital with empty arms and an empty stomach was heart wrenching. I just felt empty.

My Mum and my Husband are such great supports for me. Thank goodness they were there. They helped me to hold it all together. I was just so weak, from blood loss and emotional trauma, and just so very empty. The drive home was almost silent from what I remember. I wish now that I had thought of how he would come home, so we could have planned for it and had his seat ready for him. I wish that we had the chance to show him his room and to lie him in his cot. There will always be regrets in that way.

I spent a whole day in my office making a movie with pictures to music to be played at his funeral. I wanted to introduce him to everyone who was coming to support us. I wanted them to know how much he meant to us, how much he was wanted and how much he was and still is loved. It was so important to me.

I have birthed two healthy children since then; two perfect, active, happy and healthy children. Their labours were so peaceful, relaxed and easy, especially in comparison to Charlie's labour. It's very different to birth a child when you're ready to meet them and knowing that you will get to watch them grow up. Birthing a 'sleeping' baby means having to let them go and I was not ready for that either.

The next year, and more, was a blur of pretending to be ok, and avoiding people because it was just so tiring to pretend to be happy for them. The depression, anxiety, and lack of motivation were unshakable. It took all my energy just to drag myself out of bed. I would cry most days, just to release some of the emotion. I continued studying my Graphic Design course which gave me a purpose, but otherwise my life just felt empty.

Within the first six months, if a doctor had told me that I only had two weeks left to live, it would have been a welcome relief. It was all just too hard. I would never have hurt myself or committed suicide, but I didn't particularly want to live either. I was grieving for the person that I used to be, for the mother that I was supposed to be, for the 'purpose' that I had anticipated and wanted so badly. Then it was all gone.

I would look at other parents who were treating their kids badly and think, "Why the hell did I have to lose my son and they get to keep theirs?" The pain and anger just bubbled away. My hubby and I pulled together and supported each other, we have become stronger and more connected in many ways. We have seen the best and the worst of each other.

Friends would complain about how annoying their kids were and how they just wanted five minutes of peace and I would feel so much envy for them. I would have given anything to be sleep deprived, annoyed and frustrated. I kept thinking, why them and not me? Those things just ate away at me. But I valued their friendships to help me to 'feel normal' because on the inside I was just sad, angry, heartbroken and lost.

My first Mother's Day was the worst day of my life. Worse than Charlie's funeral, at least I could prepare mentally for that. Twelve months before, Mother's Day 2011, we found out that Charlie was 'on his way' and the following year was going to be so amazing!

But it wasn't. It was empty, quiet and all I could do all day was cry. I can understand why it is termed 'heartbroken' because the pain in my chest was exactly like something inside was being pulled apart. It physically hurt. At the end of that day, we decided that the following year, we would have something to celebrate. We stopped all contraception and decided to just 'see what happens'.

Two weeks later, Braxton was on his way. I think of him as the universe's apology for completely screwing us over the first time. At sixteen weeks into the pregnancy, we found out that we were having another little boy, and he was completely healthy, and just perfect in every way. We then announced our pregnancy to the world.

The sixteen weeks before that were incredibly stressful, trying to 'not fall in love' with this one just in case he was taken too. But that's impossible and it was an incredible relief when we found out he was healthy. We loved our kids as soon as the pregnancies were confirmed; in fact, we loved our kids when they were just a thought in our minds! I was so afraid of losing our second child that I was paranoid around sick people, avoided them like they had the plague. I only ate healthy foods and avoided all of the potentially dangerous foods, just like I did with Charlie, but this time I was anxious about it. Luckily, he is totally worth all of the fear, anxiety and insecurities around his pregnancy. I had terrible nausea with his pregnancy, the day that we found out that he was OK, that nausea went away.

We now have two little rainbows in our household. They have certainly helped to put our broken hearts back together and I am grateful for that every day. Charlie's ashes are in his bedroom, where they will stay until we are ready to move them. I have felt him watching over all of us and I truly feel that his soul is still here with us. I'm not religious but this is the feeling I have. I'm not sure what I believe about the after-life, but I have seen and felt things that I cannot explain, and that is okay with me.

WP: MULTIPLE LOSSES

I never wanted children; I was too busy enjoying my work and life travelling and having fun, being the best aunty spoiling my niece and giving her back to her mum. But then I reached thirty-nine and things changed. I can't explain it, but it happened, and I wanted a baby more than anything.

I got pregnant quickly but miscarried at around eight weeks. I don't really remember how I felt at the time and hadn't told many people, but the next pregnancy sticks in my mind.

Again, I got pregnant fairly quickly. I felt different from last time, was sick all the time but felt positive that I'd be ok. I'd told my Mum, Dad and Sister as it was my Dad's Sixtieth Birthday and I was approaching my Fortieth. Our plans were changed. I'd made my first midwife appointment and was very excited.

Several weeks on, I felt pains and knew something wasn't right. I called the doctor who told me to phone the hospital, I was passed around several departments and I felt like no one really helped. I miscarried on Mothering Sunday. I was about eleven weeks. My 'baby' was a blob in the toilet pan; I sifted it out and held it. I cried my heart out.

I had a scan to confirm that there was nothing left and remember lying on the hospital table on my own crying, feeling empty and useless. I suffered an infection in the womb following this. This resulted in me having time off work; my boss was very sympathetic. Although she didn't tell me her story, she gave hints of a similar problem.

I'd had to tell my immediate friends and family what was 'wrong with me' and they were lovely, caring and supportive, although I'm sure no one knew really what to say. My Husband cared for me whilst I cried hour after hour. I bought a necklace with the birth-stone that the baby would have had had it survived with a little trinket on it. I had no intention of ever wearing it; it sits in my jewellery box and is my only reminder.

The Oasis song *Don't Look Back in Anger* was my comfort song and I played it over and over.

Strange how we remember things like this.

I avoided friends with babies for a while. Amanda Holden lost her baby at a similar time to one of my miscarriages and it was all over the press. I am not sure if it helped at the time, but I read everything that I could about it.

At the time, I searched for bereavement helplines and called some. I was so low. At the time I believed that it just wasn't meant to be and maybe I'd left it too late to start trying.

Over the next year or so I became pregnant another three times, and each only lasted a few weeks. We saw the hospital and started tests; the problem wasn't getting pregnant it was staying pregnant, so I felt to blame. It put a strain on my marriage. I don't know what happened now, but I gave up trying. I ended up having an affair and leaving my husband a few years later.

My life would be very different had any of my babies survived, but now I am a business owner and live a fulfilling fun life with a new partner. I believe everything happens for a reason, although it's hard to think that during the heartbreak of loss.

When I think about what has helped me heal, time, friends and family all come to mind. Although Mother's Day is still a challenge, I think it will always be hard.

For anyone going through this now, please don't fear talking about your loss; there are so many people who have been through it. Time is a healer. I believe everything happens for reason even if you can't see the reason now, it may come in time.

I still get asked "Do you have children?" When I say, "No," I still feel a little awkward and that I have to justify myself (I don't tell them I've lost five, I just say I enjoy my work and travel). At a recent networking meeting a woman asked me why I didn't have *any! I couldn't think of a suitable answer at the time but the fact that she was so insensitive really upset and infuriated me.*

KD: MISCARRIAGE EXPERIENCE

I found out I was pregnant in September 2009. Myself and my Husband were incredulous, excited, nervous, clueless. We'd never experienced miscarriage or stillbirth and didn't know anyone who had so we were in a naive bubble.

Three days later and I became really ill with swine flu. My temperature was sky high and I knew this was not good news when you're pregnant. I hadn't had any symptoms so far and continued not to have any, my husband and mum insisted I was just one of the lucky ones who felt well during pregnancy, but I was desperate for any sign to confirm I was pregnant. I constantly took pregnancy tests trying to convince myself I was definitely pregnant.

We got to my twelve-week scan, six weeks later, and the sonographer said I was pregnant but not as far along as I thought. She could see an amniotic sac but there was no heartbeat yet. I just knew I wasn't pregnant any more, but I didn't know what was going on.

I kept saying it was impossible, I was sure of my dates and I must be twelve weeks and she kept insisting, "all I can tell you is what's on the screen." She asked me to go back two weeks later for another scan. We then had a period of absolute limbo. I had no symptoms. There was no heartbeat. But why hadn't I miscarried or bled? There was still that glimmer of hope, but deep down I knew it was fruitless.

A week and a half later we went bowling with some friends and when I went to the toilet I had some brown discharge. It wasn't even fresh blood, but I was so impatient with the waiting that I phoned the hospital and they asked me to go in the following morning for a scan. There was no progress from the last scan, I'd had a missed miscarriage. I felt like a fraud and I didn't know how to process it – it was still in there and had stopped growing eight weeks ago yet hadn't come out. It must have been the swine flu as the dates added up. They said I could let nature take its course or go in to hospital and have some suppositories to "bring things out". I decided on the latter as I felt like I just couldn't move forward. We hadn't told anyone at this point other than my Mum and Dad, so I suppose we didn't have the heartache of having to get in touch with friends to tell them the sad news.

Three days later I went into Harrogate Hospital. They put me on the maternity ward and I could see all the new mums and mums-to-be; I felt rubbish. They put the first lot of suppositories in and said it would take a good few hours for anything to happen, so my Husband went to do some jobs round town.

Half an hour later I stood up to go to the toilet and it felt like all my insides fell out on the floor. Everything comes away, including the wall lining so it looks horrendous and was a worrying amount of material. I had a top on but no bottoms and stood there with it all on the floor feeling so embarrassed and humiliated. I rang and rang the buzzer, and no one came, I was worried they'd put too much up there and too much had come away. I found the amniotic sac and when the nurse finally came in (a good fifteen minutes later) I handed it to her. I lost quite a lot of blood and felt very pale and sick for a few days but then just tried to move on.

How very sad it all was. I did get an apology from the ward matron about the way I was treated. It was bad enough they put me on the maternity wing but then to leave me all that time was awful.

My mum gave me some advice and it may not be for everyone, but it worked for me. She said the "more you put on it, the harder it will be to move on". If you name the baby, work out the due date, or think of when it would have had its first day at school, it's harder to process. So, I didn't do any of that.

But the fear of germs and miscarrying again stayed with me through my four subsequent pregnancies. In fact, with my most recent I had flu (even though I'd had the flu jab) at thirty weeks and convinced myself the baby would be stillborn. I refused to eat chicken in case it was under cooked and made me ill. If anyone came around to see me and told me that they'd been ill recently I would be rigid with fear.

Even when I've given birth I worry the baby is going to get ill. It's something that will never leave me, but I recognise it and don't try and cover it up. I realise I can be extremely irrational but that's the way it is.

I saw my Dad today and he's got a cold sore. I only realised after he'd been holding my twelve-week-old little boy for ten minutes and my blood ran cold. I baby-wiped him all over his face and hands (the baby not my Dad!) and when we got home I bathed him and put our clothes straight in the wash.

I don't know how people can have the strength to go through miscarriage after miscarriage. Mine was a happy ending in that I now have four lovely boys. I don't hide what happened and share my experience if it's appropriate.

When I went back to work, my boss was brilliant. She had had a stillbirth many years before and was extremely supportive. Especially in my subsequent pregnancies when I worried about everything. I work in HR now and sadly have back to work meetings with women who've been off after a miscarriage. I like to think I can say the right things and give them some comfort (if they seek it) that I had no complications with any of my subsequent pregnancies.

I don't love change. I feel anxious if plans change but I also love spontaneity and impulsiveness. Humans are complex I suppose. You have to be fairly good with change being a parent of a large family. If one of my children shows signs of getting ill I become very anxious. I didn't seek out support at the times, although wish I had. I suffer with anxiety and have had CBT where we talked about my fear of germs and illness and dying, which has helped.

I have learnt that I'm quite resilient. I've also learnt a lot about others, namely a lot of people I know have had miscarriages but it's still something not many people talk about.

If you are going through this now, know that time helps. It doesn't matter if you were four weeks or thirty-four weeks, pregnancy is a magical amazing thing and it really hurts if it doesn't work out.

EC: MULTIPLE LOSSES

I've always been sensitive to the changes in my hormones; I can tell I'm pregnant well before it can be picked up on a test. This happened when I had my first child at nineteen years old and continued for the rest of my pregnancies.

Several years after marrying my Husband, we had the first of many positive pregnancy tests. This one ended up becoming a false negative; something we weren't aware of. After weeks of getting darker and darker, one day we got a negative. A chemical pregnancy.

The next was confirmed very quickly with the doctor; my hormonal 'tells' were there again. However, at work one day, when I was approximately eight weeks pregnant, I was out to lunch with a colleague and suddenly didn't feel well and went to the loo. Brown stuff came out and I had an instant sinking feeling that something was terribly wrong. It was a big day at work as I had important time-sensitive tasks that I had to do in the evening, so would have been working late. I went to my female boss and just blurted out "I think I'm having a miscarriage." She just replied, "Are you still OK to work tonight?" Not even sit down have some water – nothing!

I was in such shock I just said yes and went straight back to work. I was under awful pressure trying to get the work done. I waited until I was finished, later that evening and got a taxi to A&E in the Maternity Hospital. I was shocked how she treated me.

I was on my own in A&E 'till my husband could get there; the staff were under a lot of pressure that night. One nurse made a flippant comment, something along the lines of at that early stage in pregnancy there's nothing we can do anyway so basically, you'll have to wait.

I was sent home and went back in for a few bloods tests to check levels over the next week, but baby was gone. I went into a bit of a depression/shock but went back to work quickly. I was pregnant again about two-months later (too quick now I feel) and was in the early pregnancy unit for lots of early, positive, scans. Knicker watch was constant!

The next scan was when I should have been thirteen-weeks pregnant. I was feeling anxious beforehand and had even started an argument with my husband before we went it. It's like I knew something was wrong.

We went in and as soon as the midwife started I knew something was up, she was shifting about, trying different buttons. I can't remember what words she said but I knew our baby had died. I let a cry out that was guttural, and the midwife got upset and left the room.

We talked over with my own doctor about options and decided on waiting to see if baby would come out without any intervention, so we went through about another three weeks of waiting. I got a bit freaked out (and I remember I hated feeling this way) about the fact that there was a dead baby inside me (that feeling still makes me so upset). Then a D&C was suggested so I went for that.

After I came around from the general anaesthetic a nurse came in and asked if we'd like to see our baby. I couldn't believe it, I didn't think after the procedure there would be anything to see. More information is needed for women on all that (I'm in Ireland though so not NHS). She brought out our tiny but perfectly formed little baby with what looked like a little smile.

Going home with a little white coffin was unreal. We named our baby, with a blessing from the priest. It was a great comfort for me to have the burial and that I can visit when I need.

Whilst I was supported during my time off work from family, my boss called and asked if I was "better yet." After returning to work, I decided to take a carer break of six-months; after what we have been through I was not coping, and the job was a highly pressured environment.

My friends were great – my best friend was having fertility issues over the years so made it very hard for both of us to deal with what I was going through, but she was always there when I really needed her.

I also went on Rollercoaster, a pregnancy website that was a fantastic support & great forum; I still chat daily with thirty or so from my group.

I always found it funny people saying at least you have your other children – you would never say that to someone who had lost a brother or sister – at least you have your other brother. I know how blessed I am too have four healthy children but that doesn't lessen any of the losses.

LG: OVERSEAS MC

I moved to the Middle East in January 2011, met my husband in 2014 and we married in 2016. In the Summer of 2016, just a few months after we got married, we found out we were pregnant. We were both delighted as I was thirty-seven and thought it would be difficult to fall pregnant.

Here in the Middle East, the doctor asks you to come for your first maternity visit between the sixth and seventh week of pregnancy. As much as I wanted to see the doctor I tried to delay the first appointment to the middle of my seventh week. The day came, and my husband and I went to visit the doctor. She had a chat with my husband and I, took some bloods for rafts of tests and then did an ultrasound. The doctor was looking for what could be interpreted as a heartbeat on the scan. She found our tiny baby, took a picture for us and quickly mentioned that she thought I may have my dates wrong.

We were due to go on holiday, discussed this with the doctor and she said, "go and enjoy yourself," so off we went to South Africa and Mauritius.

I didn't feel so well before we went on holiday, but I just put it down to a long hot summer here. As soon as I landed in South Africa and breathed some fresh clean air, I felt so much better. We had a great holiday and moved across to Mauritius for a relaxing week in the sun.

On one of our last days, we went to visit the capital of Mauritius and when we came back I started to spot a little and feel some cramps. I sent my Doctor a message and asked her advice. She just told me to rest, a few hours later I text her again. I'd started to bleed and now was in significant pain, and I knew I was miscarrying as my pregnancy symptoms had been disappearing.

I put on a brave face to go out with my husband to a posh restaurant, stopping by the local gas station to buy some sanitary towels. The waiters thought I was really bizarre as I spent most of the evening in the bathroom. We managed to get through dinner, *came back to our hotel room and I spent the rest of the night struggling in pain.*

I know people say I should have gone to the hospital, but I spoke to the hotel doctor and we both thought there was no point as it was clear I was losing our baby and I was due to return to the Middle East the following morning.

We returned home, and I went to the doctor. She gave me a scan and confirmed I had lost the baby. I was still bleeding, and I asked her my options. She told me that the tablets to speed everything up were virtually impossible to obtain here and they were only available at government hospitals. In five years of living in the Middle East, I now suddenly felt disadvantaged as a woman. Ultimately, I was OK, and I continued to miscarry naturally, however my lack of choices left me feeling disheartened.

I hadn't reached the end of the first trimester, so I hadn't really told many people, but the comments I received taught me something about how different cultures and people understand miscarriage. My cleaning lady said I miscarried either because I "didn't eat enough green mango and vinegar," or it was because I "wore high heels". I also noticed the difference between family members who would talk and listen to me for hours and others who found it uncomfortable to talk about our miscarriage and told us to move on.

One of the things I learned about miscarriage was that so many of my friends had hidden theirs. In the midst of my miscarriage I felt like a bad friend for not being there for my friends when they needed me, as well as feeling selfish that I had now shared I was having a miscarriage when they had kept it to themselves.

Around eighteen months and one chemical pregnancy later, a friend posted on Facebook with a scan picture and cute baby grow, with the usual joy that she was due in the following September. Some quick calculations and I realised that she was less than eight weeks pregnant. I read the hundreds of messages congratulating her. I was concerned, "isn't it a bit early..I hope everything goes ok". A few weeks later, she posted again to say she had a miscarriage, so I reached out to her to send my love, leaving me with all these questions about the joy and heartbreak of pregnancy, announcements and subsequent pregnancy loss.

The best I could do was to send my love and the names of mothers that I found strength from by following on Instagram. (@featheringtheemptynest and @ihadamiscarriage are two that I recommend).

This all left me wondering:

When is the right time to announce a pregnancy?

How do we talk about miscarriage?

How do we treat those parents who were parents but never met their babies?

I'm nearly forty now, realising that my fertility is decreasing, the comments from my colleagues continue; 'no baby yet?', dreading the arrival of my period and missing the feelings of hope that pregnancy can bring. The biggest thing I learned through this is the unbelievable strength of a mother's love, even without a living child.

Here's hoping for the rainbow.

JS: NOAH'S STORY

I never imagined we would be that family. The family that people wouldn't know what to say to. The family that suddenly seems broken, for whom everything seems impossible. It was on 17th July, 2015, we became that family. A day that will be etched in our memories forever.

In April 2015 at our twelve-weeks scan we found out we were having twins. The pregnancy seemed perfect. I proudly showed of my growing bump and bought the cutest outfits. Everything was faultless until the morning of 16th July. As I woke up, I went to the toilet and noticed a small amount of blood in my underwear. Little did we know that our dreams were about to be shattered. We drove to the hospital and the nurses conducted an internal examination and informed us that I was over four-cm dilated. Our boys were on their way.

After this point, nothing seemed real.

Our beautiful twin boys were born on 16th July 2015 at just 25 +5. Oscar weighed 1lb 12ozs and Noah weighed 1lb 10ozs. I remember thinking they were both just so beautiful and perfect.

We spent the next thirty hours being "normal" proud parents. Friends and family congratulated us.

But, on Friday 17th July 2015, our beautiful Noah lost his fight for life. He lived for just thirty hours.

We never considered losing either of our boys was a possibility. So, when a nurse told us that we needed to hold our boy to say goodbye our whole world stopped. We held Noah and told him repeatedly how much we loved him and how much we wanted him. We watched his heart stop beating and our hearts broke.

Whilst coping with Oscar in intensive care, we were also planning Noah's funeral. It was so difficult, especially as our Facebook feeds reminded us of friends that had been pregnant at the same time and were planning their baby's christenings, as we were planning Noah's funeral. It did not seem fair, and this was not how it was supposed to be.

I remember being told by a consultant, "Do not plan Noah's funeral yet in case you have to plan another funeral for Oscar".

We have gained friends and lost friends along the way. I remember the awkwardness. Friends told us that the simple action of buying a card was difficult. They didn't know if they should buy a card to say, "congratulations on the birth of your twins", "congratulations on the birth of your baby" or "sorry to hear of your loss". I think one of the hardest things a family member said was "at least you have one."

The best advice I can give around friends and family is to recognise they also feel your loss and are worried they will say the wrong thing, or do the wrong thing, and make it worse. My husband and I were very honest with our friends and said "nothing they can do can make this any worse. We would rather they say the wrong thing they say nothing at all." This helped to break the fear and our friends and family were able to provide us with the support we needed.

Oscar spent twelve weeks in hospital and during those weeks I felt I was not able to grieve for Noah. I cried but I had no option but to be strong for Oscar. It was when we went home that the reality of what had happened to us really affected me. I struggled and felt isolated from those around me.

Losing Noah very nearly broke me. I think one of the hardest feelings for me is the sense of failure. I believe it was my role as a mother to keep my boys safe and I felt I had failed.

It was six months after losing Noah that I found the courage to admit I needed help. I visited my doctors and completely broke down. It was the first time I felt I was able to let go of everything inside and say, "this isn't right, and I am not coping". I was offered anti-depressants and referred to Healthy Minds for talking therapies. I refused the anti-depressants as I wanted to talk about my emotions and what had happened first.

There was another six weeks to be seen by a Healthy Minds Counsellor. I vividly remember parking for my assessment and wanting to scream and run, this wasn't what I had planned. However, I gathered myself and sat in front of a stranger and again poured my heart out. I was honest about how much I was struggling and the impact this was having on my life. After fourty-five minutes I was informed Healthy Minds wasn't the right service for me as I needed bereavement counselling. I was offered Cruse's number to self-refer myself but there was a six-month waiting list. I felt cheated. I had used every ounce of energy I had to attend that appointment and I felt like the door had been closed and I was exhausted.

I decided I would have to cope on my own because I couldn't face another door closing. However, my friends knew I wasn't coping and encouraged me to contact Edward's Trust. I was reluctant, but I made an appointment.

I remember my first counselling session. I was shaking and as I walked into the room I sobbed, "I don't want to be here. This is not the place I ever wanted to be." The counsellor listened to me and after the first session she arranged my bereavement support and I felt such a huge sense of relief and that someone understood and was prepared to help me. Edward's Trust helped to put me back together. They allowed me to talk about the guilt I felt and helped me to develop coping strategies.

Our journey changed all of us, nothing will ever be the same. However, we realised that we can't change what happened, but we can use our experiences to support others to really make a difference.

I created Noah's Star.

Noah's Star is a sibling support service which has been set up especially for the brothers and sisters of babies receiving neonatal care. The service, which is run by volunteers, provides engaging activities and supervised play for children, so that their parents can spend time and attend to their newborns. It is one of the first organised sibling support service within the UK. We currently have a team of forty volunteers and have provided over seven hundred and fifty hours of support at the Neonatal Intensive Care Unit at Birmingham Women's Hospital since we launched in October 2017.

I have survived, and I feel stronger. It was important for me to be honest with my friends and family, so they could support me; to gain professional support from the counsellors at Edward's Trust and to find a way to use my grief in a positive manner, creating Noah's Star. These are the things that helped me to heal.

SB: EARLY LOSS / FERTILITY

I didn't know I was pregnant when I experienced my miscarriage, but we had been trying to get pregnant for over six months; we already had a three-year-old. I went to the doctor because we weren't getting pregnant and I'd been bleeding for over three weeks. The Dr took bloods and forty-eight hours later rang me to tell me I was pregnant; at least I had hCG in my blood. I was sent to the early pregnancy unit and spent all day waiting for further blood tests with no one telling us anything.

Later in the day I was called into a room and told by a doctor that my levels had dropped. I was no longer pregnant, but it was very early, so I shouldn't worry. I froze and then ran out of the room – the staff weren't great and told my Husband I had to come back every day for further blood tests until my levels dropped but I knew I couldn't step into there again.

Interestingly about ten weeks before, I HAD felt pregnant and had a much lighter bleed than usual, and a week into my three-weeks of bleeding I felt like I had passed something. So, when I went back to the GP the next day she calculated I was actually about eight weeks pregnant when I miscarried. She was amazing and agreed that I could have my follow up tests at the GP surgery as she understood I didn't want to go back to the hospital. It took nearly three weeks for my HCG levels to drop back down.

My work was amazing; I had a week off and when I went back everyone was supportive. My husband's family was great, my family less so. I spent a lot of time on Miscarriage Association forums sharing my feelings and found that helped. I also wrote out my story for myself so that I could move on from it.

I was lucky and was pregnant again two-months later. I was terrified this time and had a private early scan so that I could be sure all was well. It was, and my Rainbow Baby is now five-years old. This helped me heal and I also had an energy releasing session a couple of years later where I fully let go of my miscarried baby.

For anyone going through this, take it one day at a time. Remember it isn't your fault (I blamed myself and my body a lot), Journal and Meditate. Finally, get support from others, it's easy to keep quiet about what has happened, but I found that in sharing with others it helped a lot and I also discovered that quite a few friends had similar experiences but also didn't really share.

LG - JACK'S STORY

On 27th July 2014, at thirty-seven weeks pregnant our precious baby boy, was sadly born sleeping. He had blonde hair, long legs and it was by far the most heart-breaking experience of my life. We named him Jack William Goodway, he was 6lb 2oz and his beautiful memory will live on in our hearts forever.

The support I received from my community midwife and the midwives on shift was exceptional. They were kind, caring, and sympathetic, nothing was ever too much trouble for them. I'd built up a really good relationship with my Community Midwife, Claire, during the whole of my second pregnancy with Jack, she also then went on to be my community midwife through my subsequent pregnancy and the arrival of our little rainbow boy; Archie Jack Goodway. Claire went on to be shortlisted as 'Midwife of the Year' from my nomination at the National RCM Awards (Royal College of Midwives) in March 2016. I will never forget the *support she gave me, she was a real source of comfort and gave me hope for the future.*

During the most difficult day of my life at 2.37am on Sunday 27th July 2014 I endured the most, devastating, heart-breaking and unimaginable experience and somehow managed to deliver my beautiful little sleeping Jack. The midwives and student midwives on shift that looked after me during this awful time (whose names I will remember for ever: Ellie and Melissa) were kind, caring, compassionate and cried tears along with me, as I know it was such a heart-breaking experience for them too. They made sure we spent time with Jack, took photographs of him and made sure he was in the best care possible. Nothing was ever too much trouble for them during this unbearable weekend, which will haunt me forever.

The morning after I delivered my perfect little boy, a consultant approached our room with a post-mortem form and gave it to me and my hubby to fill in. This was really difficult to comprehend as I was still high on morphine and just utterly empty, numb and destroyed. How on earth could I sign my life away to something that I was still in shock about and had no concept of making any decisions? Melissa, sat down on the settee in our room and comforted us, explained everything and made the whole process bearable, she did this with tears rolling down her cheeks. I will also never forget that one year later, on 2nd June, the day my rainbow baby arrived into the world, Ellie (who delivered Jack) heard I was on the ward and came to find me to carry out Archie's first checks. She hugged me, we talked about her memories of Jack and we cried together. We also smiled together with emotion as I had my rainbow boy to hug that bit tighter that evening.

I had been a Head of Girls PE in a Secondary School for twelve years. I got pregnant with my first daughter back in 2012, who arrived into the world after my waters broke on the netball court, and within 20 minutes of arriving to the hospital. My first pregnancy was a dream, I was still skinny old me, with a netball up my top. I was glowing with excitement and felt great during the whole forty-one weeks I carried her. The other staff at school referred to me as an "Ambassador for pregnant women," nothing changed, no extra risk assessment, no special chairs or reduced timetables, and not one day off sick during the whole nine months!

As soon as my little netballer, Nell, arrived into the world I fell in love; she was my baby, my best friend who smiled all day and slept all night. I loved being a mommy from the off! I was super excited to discover I was pregnant with our second child in December 2013 and couldn't wait to see how another child would enhance our perfect little family. As always, everyone at school knew I would just coast through the pregnancy as I did first time, which I did. I supported our whole school sports day, had a full teaching timetable, mentored trainee teachers and ran every possible extra-curricular club possible. I broke up from school for the summer holidays on Fri 18th July at thirty-six weeks pregnant. I was excited about the six-weeks off with my little girl and then preparing for baby Number Two's arrival on the 19th August 2014.

Within just one week later at thirty-seven weeks, our whole world came crashing down on us. How could this be? Things like this don't happen to families like us. How will life ever be the same again? How will we survive this?

After experiencing the worst day of my life and delivering my beautiful little sleeping baby boy into the world (you think labour is physically painful, try delivering a baby that has died, the emotional pain that goes alongside this is truly unbearable, it makes me shudder to think I actually did it!) And then having to return home after the worst weekend of my life to be greeted with florist vans, with so many bouquets and cards that just kept on coming from family, friends, colleagues, my netball team, Dean's cricket team, neighbours; everybody was just in shock and heartbroken for us.

By 14th September my Head Teacher from school made a special visit to come and see how we were and if there was anything he could do to help. This was really comforting, not that I could make conversation with him without crying, Dean had to do all the talking. I just sat there in a trance, still not really knowing what was going on. Mr Wilkes was always a lovely, thoughtful Head Teacher who cared about his staff, he told me to not worry about school for a while and to take as much time as was needed and to do what was best for us. We were totally honest with him and suggested that this whole experience was life changing and regardless of what the future held I would not be returning to teaching full-time.

Just before we left the hospital after delivering Jack, Dean had said: "Next time we're here, it's going to be on much happier circumstances, I promise you" followed by a massive hug with lots and lots of tears. My two-year-old little girl and Dean were about the only thing that kept me going, some days I could've just walked, and I dread to think where I may have ended up.

Growing up in a girl-heavy family was something I always cherished. My Mom and Dad had three daughters and six granddaughters. My Dad was hoping that one day very soon there would be a "blue one" welcomed into our family. I do always worry about my Dad because I think it had a bigger impact on him than what many people would've realised, he was so close to getting his first grandson but yet, so far. The loss of a child has a major impact on the whole family. My Mom, Dad, Dean's Mom, Dean's brothers' family, my two Sisters and their families (who I am really close to) were just truly heartbroken. They all would've done anything to take my pain away, but there is literally nothing that anyone can say that would bring Jack back. Our family unit became very important during the immediate grieving time, I would've been lost without each and every one of them.

My best friend, April, invited me to hers so that a few other friends could see me as they were so desperate to just give me a hug. I was scared to death of coming face to face with them, I knew they were devastated for me, they also knew how desperate I was to be a Mommy again, and how badly I wanted this baby. I walked into the room and we all just burst into tears, we all hugged and talked about Jack, they were amazing. A few months later they paid for me to go on a spa day together just to see me smile again. They bought me so many lovely gifts and lots of tributes to help me remember Jack. I have some truly amazing friends, and a beautiful family. I love to hear people say his name. I love to see gifts with his name on. The amount of blue letter Js that appeared around my house was very heart-warming. My special boy was always going to be with us. Every family member and close friend made sure of that.

The night before Jack's funeral, I finally felt brave enough to open his beautiful memory box I felt I needed to look at his photographs, so I could remember who I was saying goodbye to. I had really fond memories of his blonde head of hair, his long legs, and he was just the spitting image of my little girl. The days after we lost him, Nell used to toddle into our room every morning and the minute I opened my eyes to look at her, I could just see Jack's beautiful face, it was so difficult, but I have so much to thank my perfect little Nell for, and when she is old enough to truly understand this I will explain to her how she saved my life.

His photographs were beautiful but at the same time if only love could've brought him back again, I would've held him in my arms forever. I smelt the teddy bear that was in his memory box, I distinctly remember Midwife Melissa going through his memory box with us in the hospital. She explained that he also had a teddy that stayed with him, and they both smelt the same; I just smelt my teddy and cried, how on earth was this happening to us?

Why on earth was he not here with us?

I worked my way through his beautiful memory box and found a life-line in a SANDS leaflet (Stillbirth and Neonatal Death) Charity. I couldn't bring myself to read it fully, but I kept it out of his memory box and put it to one side until I felt strong enough to look into it further. Even though I quickly worked out that there were local support groups that I could attend, I remember thinking, "does this heartbreak actually happen to other people?" I just felt so alone, how on earth was I going to survive the worst time of my life? How would life ever get any better for us?

It took me two months to actually do anything with the SANDs leaflet. I managed to break the dark blur of what was going on in my life, dust my laptop off and word a very brief email about attending their next support group meeting which was taking place on Monday 1st September, I knew I had to get out of the house and do something. I had to deal with what was happening beyond my four walls, and they were just creeping in on me. Dean thought it was a good idea that I went and even though I would've preferred if he'd have come with me for the first time, I knew there was no way he could do it. He just wasn't ready to talk about Jack to a room full of strangers and I respected his wishes.

It was such a brave step for me to take but I managed to pop my satnav in the car and on auto pilot I drove to the Birmingham SANDS meeting. I pulled up and parked to the place I was hoping was the correct venue, I think I was looking for a Birmingham SANDS signpost somewhere, but the only sign I could see was for 'Edward's Trust – Supporting children and families who are facing loss and surviving bereavement' with a lovely colourful kite next to it. I thought I must've been in the right place.

I walked in feeling super nervous, and when I was met with so many other friendly faces I just cried the whole night, and I realised that all the lovely ladies that I met had been through the unimaginable too. They were still breathing, walking, smiling.

They were literally the nicest group of people I wished I'd never met. This visit was a big turning point for me, I was able to talk about my story, my beautiful little boy, my feelings of complete loss and isolation and each and every one of the befrienders sat and listened and knew exactly how I was feeling. I was so glad I made the step that night to go.

I also discovered that Birmingham SANDS hired the Edward's Trust building every month to carry out their Befriender meetings. I took some of the leaflets home to find out more. Lots of the other bereaved Mommies I'd met that night were also receiving support from Edward's Trust too, as they could offer one-to-one counselling as opposed to just group support.

I was truly never aware of any of this until the day I lost my little Jack. Why would it have come under my radar? I had no reason to know anything about baby-loss support groups. Something like that was never going to happen to somebody like me!

Time passed in a blur and before I knew it I was being dropped off by my hubby to go on a three-day retreat with Edward's Trust with three other bereaved Mommies of baby boys, a bereavement counsellor and a 'Well-Being in Bereavement' Therapist. We were whisked off to a beautiful location in Shropshire and it is here where I finally felt that I could deal with what had happened to me. I was going to survive this journey and somehow, I was going to try to turn this life-changing experience into a positive one, I was going to survive this journey and I was going to do it for my special little boy; I owed him that.

The last four-years have been an emotional rollercoaster. Right now, I should be buying Jack a School Uniform or getting his feet measured to start Reception. Instead we will all go and pick him a nice big number four balloon and a new keepsake for his forever garden. Nell and Archie will choose a cake for him and we will all sing Happy Fourth Birthday to him. Four years without him seems crazy! Four years that as time goes by, you feel further and further away from him.

What would he look like now? Would I ever recognise him? I know for a fact he would look more like his big sister Nell as opposed to his little brother Archie. Nell and Jack's newborn photographs are identical. Archie is very different, he has darker skin, dark hazel eyes and the image of his Daddy. It's difficult to imagine another little mini Nell running around the house right now.

For me, as a Mommy, Bereaved Mommy, Wife, Daughter, friend, colleague, befriender and even netballer, this whole experience has been staggering. I have learnt so much about myself and it has shaped me to be far more grateful of what I have.

I do feel blessed every single day. I wake up to a wonderful husband, two beautiful children who literally melt my heart every single day; I squeeze them so tight it hurts. They are now aged six and three; they have some understanding of their brother in Heaven and what he looked like and when he appeared in my tummy chronologically in comparison to them, but I don't think they really realise how special they are to me. I am so grateful to be a Mommy to them, but I am also very proud to be a Mommy to my little Jack. He has shaped my life, he has made me look at things differently and I am very grateful of the path he has now put me on.

My job has now changed, I no longer teach PE in a Secondary School. I felt very lonely in a Classroom surrounded by thirty teenagers, on the outside I was trying to pretend everything was OK I was still Mrs Goodway, Head of Girl's PE, but inside I was crumbling. I couldn't do it anymore, I needed to work with adults who had some understanding or consideration of what I had been through, and for me a job at Edward's Trust as the Engagement Coordinator shone through. I now get to meet Mommies/parents like me every day at Edward's Trust.

I see them at the start of their journey and I get to see them grow and survive their awful heartbreak. I get to see how grateful they are to have received help from Edward's Trust and then, when they feel strong enough, they often contact me to make a difference to our work and support the volunteering and fundraising team. This in itself is far more rewarding for me as a bereaved Mom and a member of the team now at Edward's Trust. Edward's Trust helped to 'save my life' and drag me from the depths of despair.

I feel truly grateful that Jack has given me this opportunity to make a difference to others, to think differently, to feel differently and to appreciate life after it has sent you down a different path. A path you would never wish for but a path that cannot be changed. A parent isn't supposed to bury their own child! Continue to fly high and shine bright little boy.

HS- MISCARRIAGE

My story is about our miscarriage back in April 2009. It was a much wanted and planned pregnancy. Although slightly against advice, and our better judgement, we had started telling people at about eight weeks due to a serious health scare with my Husband's Father. Telling the family that we were pregnant provided hope and smiles at a frantic time in the hospital.

About five weeks later, we were out walking with friends and their dog, I clearly remember being cautious of the dog (a huge Great Dane) and slipping on rocks and swinging gates etc. We stopped at a pub for a cool drink at the end of the walk and I went to the loo. I found blood. My husband and I went to A&E and we were immediately admitted as by now I was losing lots of blood. I cannot describe the feeling – numb panic is the best I can come up with. Every time I went to the loo I was given a container which the nurses then duly checked through and kept assuring me it was 'just blood'. We were there for a number of hours and although we kept being given well-intentioned hope, I think I knew it was over. There was just so much blood.

Later we were moved to the neonatal unit and a young, smart and extremely kind and sensitive doctor apologised that my pregnancy had ended and that a procedure was needed to remove what was remaining in my uterus. He was so patient and did not rush us out of the room despite it being a very busy department. I can still remember the exact physical feeling of the 'removal' today. We left later in a state of shock. Cruelly, my miscarriage had occurred on my Mum's birthday.

We immediately went home, and I insisted on sleeping in the guest room in the attic – I just couldn't face our own bed. We held each other and cried a lot. I slept a lot and generally hid from the world for months. Looking back, it was some sort of major emotional breakdown. My husband was amazing. Despite it also being his loss, he returned to work and brought me food and drink. I did not want to see or speak to anyone except him. Not even my mother. I stayed in my attic.

I had my own consultancy service and my husband phoned and emailed all my clients stating I wouldn't be back. I had told most of them the previous week that I was pregnant, and they had all been so excited and lovely – I guess they added it all up to work out what had gone wrong. Up to that point I had never been late or absent for any client. I received some very kind emails. Most of which (I am ashamed to say now) I could not find the words to reply to – even to this day. As someone who always took pride in professionalism, I find this quite difficult, even now.

I don't recall what eventually brought me out of my hiding place and I couldn't say what date it was.

Not long after my miscarriage, my Sister fell pregnant with twins. She told me as sensitively and carefully as she could, but my heart broke again. I tried so hard to sound happy for her, but the pain was so immense, and I broke down for hours after the call. I felt robbed. How awful to admit that (especially my own sister's good news) but that's how it felt.

I am very grateful and felt I was treated well at the hospital. A very busy midwife left a leaflet for me at the reception which at the time I was angry about – I felt I had been dropped like a hot stone now I was no longer carrying any baby. But like so many in the NHS she was rushed off her feet. Actually, the leaflet was for a Miscarriage Helpline which I did call and found extremely helpful and supportive.

There were so many things said that were meant to be supportive. The usual, "you're still young, there's still time, there will be other pregnancies," when you just want to scream, "BUT I WANTED THIS PREGNANCY." The very worst was, "it is nature's way. If it had carried on, you might have had a little monster." Unbelievable!

The number one thing that helped me was talking. Sharing. Speaking to people who understood. Finding out how common it is and how it should not be a taboo subject. That you're not alone in this most personal and painful type of grief. And it is a real grief. At whatever stage it comes. Grief of what was – of what could have been – and what will now not be. I didn't go to any group support or counselling, but did use support phonelines, which helped.

Time also helped me heal; and my husband. Talking to one particular friend who was going through the same thing at about the same time. Having my two children (2010 and 2013). Although they are *never* replacements. My husband and I have a private nickname for our lost child and we occasionally talk about him/her and have a little cathartic cry. This does help.

I am sad to say that some family members did not help at all. They still shush me and shake their heads at me if I try to talk about it. Obviously for some this is an inappropriate topic of conversation. That is why I was so moved by this project (Clara's Book); a chance to talk about it.

I was asked how I deal with change since the miscarriage and I had not linked the two before now. I guess there are fewer more painful things. Generally, I deal with change better, but not perfectly. I find that I have lost trust in my body. It failed me. I failed. I lost. We lost. It's as if I am anticipating it to fail again in the future...every day. I have learnt that I cannot control everything. And that my husband is my rock.

My guidance for anyone going through this now is to talk about it. Talk about it. Talk about it. You are not alone. It is a sad but real fact of creating life/reproduction that some potential lives are lost. It is cruel and unfair, and you are right to grieve. Allow yourself to grieve. Ignore the comments of others unless they are positive and comforting. Talk about it. Cry. Talk about it. You'll never forget, but time will start to heal. Sorry – it's a cliché – but I have found it to be true. This event in my life (despite being relatively early) was as painful as losing my dad due to cancer – and this comment seems to shock people immensely – but it was.

Perhaps this kind of project will start to challenge the taboo of talking about miscarriage, stillbirth and death shortly after birth.

ABOUT THE AUTHOR

Clara Wilcox is a Career Coach and Mentor, who lives in the West Midlands with her Husband, two children, two cats, chocolate obsession and book collection.

After growing up in North Birmingham, she gained her degree in Psychology at the University of Leicester. Her fascination with what makes people tick has continued through her career; she has been working in the career coaching and recruitment space since 2001.

She became one of the 'one in four' in 2009, after a missed, or silent, miscarriage, then experienced the devastation of the late loss of her little boy in 2010, due to Bilateral Renal Agenesis. Having got through the other side of such a devastating experience, she decided to start The Balance Collective, a social enterprise that supports parents in all their work choices, to find work to enjoy not endure.

Never afraid to speak about difficult topics, she made it her mission to be honest about her journey to becoming a Mum of two, frequently discussing her losses and its impact on her life and career outlook. She has found many of her clients have also experienced a difficult path to parenthood and were intrigued about her approach to mental health and parenting after loss.

The results of these conversations and research became *What Now?* An honest reflection on the realities of life after loss and is Clara's first book.

SUPPORT NETWORKS

There are a range of support networks, local, national and online, that can help you through your loss.

The Miscarriage Association

Pregnancy loss information and support. Offering online information, helpline and support groups.

www.miscarriageassociation.org.uk

The Pinks N Blues CIC

Offer one to one and group support to anyone who has experienced loss of their baby in the first or second trimester of pregnancy.

www.thepinksnblues.co.uk

SANDS (Stillbirth and Neonatal Death Charity)

SANDS work to support anyone affected by the death of a baby; improve the care bereaved parents receive; and create a world where fewer babies die

www.sands.org.uk

ARC (Antenatal Results and Choices)

Here for parents through antenatal screening and it's consequences

www.arc-uk.org

Tommy's

Funding research, saving babies' lives

www.tommys.org.uk

Lily Mae Foundation

Supporting parents and families after Stillbirth, Neonatal Death or Medical Termination

www.lilymaefoundation.org

Edward's Trust

Edward's Trust... Birmingham based charity supporting children and families facing loss and surviving bereavement, since 1989.

Edward's Trust is a voluntary organisation who relies solely on the generosity of our supporters. We support around 600 families' year and around three-thousand family members. In order to continue our services, we need around £600,000 per year to continue. We are always on the lookout for new ways to continue to support bereaved families.

www.edwardstrust.org.uk

THANK YOU

This is a book I really wish I couldn't have written, but I am so proud that I have. This book has been nearly a decade in the making, and the fact that I can sit here and write it shows how important these people have been in the process.

This is a collective effort, of emotional support, practical support, and a right royal kick up the arse accountability. The phrase "*Thank You*" doesn't seem enough, but it is a great start. So, in no particular order:

Thank you to Kate Dyson and Alison McGarragh-Murphy, Founder and Editor of *The Motherload,* who gave me the first wider platform to write openly about the impact of baby and pregnancy loss. They seem to appreciate my sarcastic and tongue in cheek approach!

To the team within Coffee with Dan. To Dan Meredith for becoming my "Hairy Godmother" and connecting me to Gina Cox-Roberts (for cover design) Colette Mason (for book coaching and technical wizardry), to Chloe Ivy Rose Smith (for editing and proofing). To Lucy Dowson who took my vision and created the "blurb" you will find on the back of the book.

To Monica Douglas-Clark, Chloe Thompson-Booth, and Keri Jarvis (Do It Like a Mother) and Lucy Goodway at Edwards Trust, who have not only contributed to the book's content, but have been my cheerleaders behind the scenes!

To the wonderful women that shared their baby loss stories with me. I never wanted this to be my story and mine alone; your willingness to be open and transparent will help generations, I am sure.

To my friends who have helped me over the years, especially when I was in my darker moments, but also my more recent friends that have encouraged me to get this book written. Charlotte Shutt for *telling me* the book needs to be out there and Catherine McLennan from Pink & Blues, who has always been there for me, since our original meeting in a Birmingham Coach Station Café back in 2016.

To Edward's Trust, who are not only my inspiration for the book but the support that started piecing me back together. It will come as no surprise that the proceeds of this book will be donated to the charity to continue their life-changing and lifesaving work.

Finally, to my wonderful family; my Husband Scott, who has been my rock through the worse time of our lives. To my girls, who have kept joy in my life, and to my parents and extended family and friends, who have always stood by us.

So, in closing, Thank You is not enough. Instead, I say:

Bless You, Much Obliged, Cheers, Ta, I OWE YOU ONE.

KEEP IN TOUCH

I hope you have found this book useful and will support your through your journey.

The change in perspective after our losses led me to set up a business focused on supporting people to create a work-life balance that works for them. Working predominately, but not exclusively, with parents, I use my new view on life, and over fifteen years of recruitment and leadership, to coach and mentor individuals and businesses on careers, returning to work, business and confidence.

When you are ready to connect, here is how!

Join me in my Facebook Group: "The Balance Collective with Clara Wilcox"

Follow me on Social Media: www.facebook.com/flexibleworkingforall

LinkedIn: Clara Wilcox

Twitter: @clarawilcox

Blog: www.thebalancecollective.co.uk/blog

Please feel free to share your stories with me. I'd love to hear from how the book has helped you. Here's my email address:

hello@thebalancecollective.co.uk

You don't have to go through this alone; let's stay in touch.

Clara

REFERENCES

ONE: DODGING FERTILITY BULLETS

"Polycystic Ovary Syndrome is ..."

https://www.nhs.uk/conditions/polycystic-ovary-syndrome-pcos/

TWO: THE BULLSHIT TWELVE-WEEK RULE

"seventy-five percent of miscarriages happen in the first three months"

https://www.tommys.org/our-organisation/charity-research/pregnancy-statistics/miscarriage

FOUR: LET'S TALK ABOUT GRIEF

" ...grief when you lose something important to you"

https://www.nhs.uk/Livewell/emotionalhealth/Pages/Dealingwith-loss.aspx

"symptoms of grief"

https://www.goodtherapy.org/learn-about-therapy/issues/grief

"Growing Around Grief"

http://www.loistonkin.com/growing-around-grief.html

"Dual Model of Grief"

https://whatsyourgrief.com/dual-process-model-of-grief/

"when someone we care about dies ..."

https://www.cruse.org.uk/traumatic-bereavement/traumatic-loss

"Post-Traumatic Growth"

http://www.apa.org/monitor/2016/11/growth-trauma.aspx

"People develop a better understanding ..."

http://www.apa.org/monitor/2016/11/growth-trauma.aspx

"Monica Douglas-Clark"

https://www.rebelrev.net/

"(Znoj 2016, Calhoun, Tedeschi, Cann and Hanks 2010)"

https://www.psychologicabelgica.com/articles/abstract/10.5334/pb-50-1-2-125/

"Grief Works, Julia Samuels"

https://griefworks.co.uk/

"The Light of Death, Tim Freke"

http://timfreke.com/Product/114/in-the-light-of-death

"Life After Loss, Bob Deits"

http://www.lifeafterlossonline.com/

FIVE: MENTAL HEALTH AS A BEREAVED PARENT

"Carl Rogers"

https://www.bapca.org.uk/about/carl-rogers.html

"A Mindfulness Guide for the Frazzled, Ruby Wax"

http://www.rubywax.net/frazzled.html

"Headspace App"

https://www.headspace.com/

"EMDR"

https://www.aberdeenpsychology.co.uk/emdr-trauma.php

"Exercise helps grief"

https://fitness.mercola.com/sites/fitness/archive/2014/06/27/exercise-grief.aspx

SIX: A FAMILY GRIEVING

"We were going to have a baby, but had an Angel instead"

https://www.amazon.co.uk/Were-Gonna-Have-Angel-Instead/dp/0972424113

Seven: Time to say goodbye to grief

"The As If Principle, Richard Wiseman"

https://www.amazon.co.uk/If-Principle-Radically-Approach-Changing/dp/1451675054

Eight: Returning to work as a bereaved parent

"twenty-five percent of pregnancies end in miscarriage"

https://www.tommys.org/our-organisation/charity-research/pregnancy-statistics/miscarriage

Nine: Pregnancy after loss

"one in ten-thousand births"

https://assets.publishing.service.gov.uk/government/uploads/system/uploads/attachment_data/file/398581/Bilateral_renal_agenesis__BRA__-_HP_-_FASP76.pdf

"A Rainbow Baby"

http://www.kickscount.org.uk/rainbow-baby/

"Woo-woo..."

https://en.oxforddictionaries.com/definition/woo-woo

"Do It Like A Mother"

https://www.doitlikeamother.co.uk/

Ten: returning to work with a rainbow baby

"The Motherload"

https://the-motherload.co.uk/

Eleven: The babies that come afterwards

"Potter's Baby get kidney from her Father"

http://people.com/celebrity/congresswomans-miracle-baby-gets-a-kidney-from-her-dad/

Manufactured by Amazon.ca
Bolton, ON

10934984R00103